Crocheted & Fabric Tapestry Rugs

OTHER TITLES BY THE AUTHOR

Rugmaker's Handbook Series:
#1 Knitted Rag Rugs for the Craftsman
#2 Fabulous Rag Rugs from Simple Frames
#3 Crocheted & Fabric Tapestry Rugs

Other titles:
Traditional Shirred and Standing Wool Rugs
Bohemian Braid Rugs for the Beginner
Multi-strand Braids for Flat-Braided Rugs
Flat Wrap Rugs and Baskets
Introduction to Patched Rugs
Amish Knot Rugs
Broomstick Rugs
Chain Braid Rugs
Wagon Wheel Rugs
Anchored Loop Rugs (American Locker Hooking with Rags)
Bodkin Rugs
Introduction to Tambour Rugs
Knotted Shag Rugs
Pjonging and the Single Strand Chain Braids
"Hook Braided" Rugs; the Two-strand Attached Chain Braid
Kitchen Table Rugs
String Crochet Rugs
Primitive Rug Hooking, An Introduction
"Beaded" Rugs, A Unique Standing Wool Rug
A Rugmaker's Sampler

Rugmaker's Handbook No. 3

Crocheted & Fabric Tapestry Rugs

written and illustrated by,
Master Rugmaker
Diana Blake Gray

Rafter-four Designs
Cocolalla, Idaho

Rugmaker's Handbook No. 3
Crocheted and Fabric Tapestry Rugs

Rafter-four Designs

For information address:
Rafter-four Designs
P O Box 40
Cocolalla, ID 83813
http://www.rugmakershomestead.com

including information from:
Crocheted Rag Rugs for the Beginner, Copyright 1984 by Diana Blake Gray
Crocheted Rag Rugs in Special Shapes, Copyright 1985 by Diana Blake Gray
Introduction to Fabric Tapestry Rugs, Copyright 1985 by Diana Blake Gray
Crocheted & Fabric Tapestry Rugs, Copyright 1996 by Diana Blake Gray

ISBN: 1-931426-29-5

Printed in the United States of America

Dedication

To

Floyd and Connie Blake

You're simply the best!

With love.

Contents

Handbook (con't.)

Acknowledgements

This book would have been a lesser project were it not for the thousands of rug makers who have asked questions over the past twenty-four years since the publication of my first book on crocheted rugs.

My thanks to every one of you.

Using this Book

This book is devoted to teaching the techniques of standard crocheted and fabric tapestry rugs. Each shape of crocheted rug is presented in the order of its complexity. The round shape is covered first, since it is the basic shape and is modified to make all of the other shapes. Begin with a round hotpad with standard crochet to become familiar with handling fabric strip. From that point, you can proceed to the other shapes or take on a round hotpad with fabric tapestry.

The fabric tapestry patterns are graded from beginner, through novice and intermediate to advanced techniques. You will find it easiest to work at least one pattern at the beginner and novice levels before attempting some of the fancier patterns. This sounds like a long process, but, for example if you wanted to make the "Star of Bethlehem" rug on the cover, begin with a round hotpad, then a small pinwheel (beginner) design which will then transform into the center of a diamond pattern (novice). From that point, you can start a novice level star which is also the center of a Star of Bethlehem rug.

The "handbook" at the end of the book is a general reference with fabric characteristics, requirements, and special techniques for particular effects.

INTRODUCTION

Rag rugs have been crocheted for at least 150 years in North America, but since crochet was a common household skill, early directions for the making of crocheted rugs were on the order of "just crochet with the stuff." A sample of that type of directions from the *American Farm Journal* in 1871:

"If one has plenty of old delaines or thin woolen goods, she may tear them in strips a half inch wide and knit them on coarse wooden needles or crochet them with a large crochet needle, and arrange the different colors tastefully…"

Similarly, *The Woman's Book*, published by Woman's Home Companion in 1907 gives directions:
"Having collected about twenty-five pounds of flannel rags and having dyed them the desired shades they must now be torn into strips about an inch wide, and these must be neatly sewn together, overlapping about half an inch, so that the joining is strong. Now procure a length of clothesline rope, and commence to crochet the flannel strips over the rope. This is begun in the center, like any crochet wheel for a chair back…"

Most early crocheted rugs were relatively crude as in this example from Amy Mali Hicks "The Craft of Hand-Made Rugs" 1914

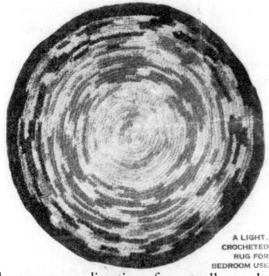

A LIGHT.
CROCHETED
RUG FOR
BEDROOM USE

Crocheted rugs were also featured in women's publications like this example from "Plain and Fancy Needlework" (June 1917).

There were no directions for actually crocheting the rug, only discussions of the fabrics and colors used in them. However, the history of crocheted rugs is indicated by the author's introduction: "Of all the hand-made rugs of our grandmothers days, now so popular again, some of the most interesting are the crocheted rugs; and they are perhaps the most durable, as no thread is used in the making."

In "Handmade Rugs" by Ella Shannon Bowles (1927), the rug below is described as being crocheted over "binding twine."

Her directions for crocheting a rug are: "Start with a chain of three...and in the first stitch make seven single crochet stitches. Crochet around and around this centre, increasing enough to keep the work flat and perfectly circular in shape."

During the same period, crocheted rugs were also made with recycled stockings instead of rags. The stockings had a built-in stretch and resilience so that they acted like yarns and held their shape with rugs. Examples of the stocking rugs surviving show the perfectly symmetrical shape of the yarn patterns and many are still in use after many decades.

CROCHETED STOCKING RUG

Hᴇʀᴇ ɪs a lovely bedroom rug made of old silk stockings dyed turquoise blue and gold.

Size   27" in diameter.

To prepare materials   The first step is to dye the stockings. There are many particularly beautiful colors to be had in silk dyes — batik dyes are especially recommended.

It is likely that your collection of stockings will be in several shades of one color, so that when they are dyed, they will vary in tone. This will give added attractiveness to the rug.

Cut each stocking into one long bias strip, starting at the top, as in diagram. When cutting, make allowance for difference in weight of stocking. Cut thin stockings 3" wide; cut heavier stockings narrower so that the "strips" will be of uniform thickness. Sew stocking strips together and wind into a ball.

Directions   The whole rug is done in single crochet. Begin with 3 chain stitches and join with a slip stitch to form a ring. Crochet 6 rows of turquoise, 1 gold, 2 turquoise, 5 gold, 8 turquoise, and 4 gold. To add a new color, simply sew it to the old.

Be sure to add enough stitches on each row, in order to enlarge the circle properly.

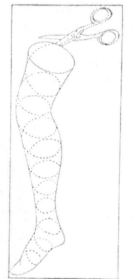

The complete directions for a depression-era crocheted rug made from stockings. Note the spiral cutting.

Rag rugs using the fabric tapestry technique were much rarer, and the fabrics to create patterns were hand-dyed. The rug below from Amy Mali Hicks "The Craft of Handmade Rugs" (1914) was the first one I came across. Seeking further information, I contacted the Smithsonian Institution in Washington, D.C.

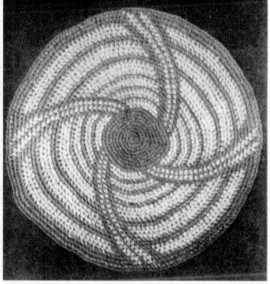

I was surprised to find that the Hicks' rug was also the only fabric tapestry rug that they could find. The directions that Hicks gives for the rug use a variable increase pattern. Apparently Hicks was an accomplished rug maker and created the rug by "feel" and wrote the directions as she worked.

Later, I did come across another fabric tapestry rug of an oval shape (below) in "Plain and Fancy Needlework" magazine (June, 1917). The accompanying article did not mention the technique or give any directions, simply labeling the rug "A design crocheted of harmonious colors."

By the 1930s and 1940s, a new strategy for creating a reliable rug pattern developed. Directions specified that fabric strips for rugs be cut on the bias so that the strips would stretch and behave similarly to yarns. Then, standard yarn patterns could be used for rugs. In the end, however, the bias-cut fabric strips continued to stretch after the rug was made and especially when it was washed. The rugs stretched out of shape permanently and became relegated to barns, attics and basements.

There are two basic strategies to crochet rugs with fabric strip. The earliest and easiest was to treat fabric strip just as if it were yarn and crochet a rug back-and-forth in rows using single or double crochet stitches. These rugs work reasonably well with thin fabric strip (one inch or less) and the problem of keeping the rug laying flat was avoided.

The second group of crocheted rug constructions are worked in rounds and referred to as "radial" patterns. These rugs are actually made as a continuous spiral and since each round makes the rug larger, extra stitches need to be added regularly to allow the rug to lie flat. It is these types of rugs that cause the most difficulty since the increase patterns which worked so reliably with yarns (six extra stitches per round) simply did not work with heavier fabric strip.

Writers of rug making directions adopted various strategies to get around the problem. Some just avoided it entirely by directing the rug maker to "increase as necessary to make the rug lie flat." That left the rug maker on her own to develop a technique that worked. She learned to crochet rugs by "feel"—if the rug began to cup she'd add more stitches. These rugs sometimes were regularly shaped with tight stitching simply because the rug maker had had a lot of practice working with fabric strip. Quite a few of these old rugs have survived from the early to mid-1900s.

Even the notable Ami Mali Hicks, who first published the technique of fabric tapestry, could only give the most general advice about crocheted rugs. Her 1914 book, *The Craft of Handmade Rugs* directs: "Double the stitches occasionally in these first rounds, just enough to keep the center of the rug from 'cupping' but not enough to make it 'full up.'…doubling takes place a regular intervals and always comes in the longest count of each round."

Some of the rugs "made by feel" became the basis for written directions. If a rug looked good, it was dissected and the stitch pattern written down. Unfortunately, when someone else tried to reproduce the effect, most often the result was not at all satisfactory, since these patterns were specific to the exact material in the original rug and the personal touch of the rug maker.

When I began researching rug structures, even contemporary sources such as Better Homes and Gardens ("Rug Making", 1978) were still publishing directions for crocheted rugs saying "increase as necessary" which was not useful. I really had expected to be able to pick up any basic needlework guide and find directions for crocheting rag rugs. It astonished me that there simply were none.

Rug yarn manufacturers could offer reliable results for making rugs with their products and published numerous pamphlets of directions. Why the yarn patterns didn't work with fabric strip puzzled me. So, as an experienced crocheter, I moved confidently forward thinking that I could certainly "increase as neccessary." I began with a yarn pattern, and as it began to cup, I added increases. Then the rug began to wave, so fewer increases...The result I dubbed "The Sombrero Syndrome."

In the early 1980s, I began to conduct experiments with fabric strip for crocheted rugs to determine why the old radial patterns did not work like they did with rug yarns. The first fact I discovered was that fabric strip—even when cut on the bias—simply does not act the same way as yarns do. Straight-cut fabric strip has no "give" and, while bias-cut fabric will stretch out, it doesn't have the resilience to resume its original shape.

It took some years experimenting with straight-cut fabric strip, but eventually I did develop a standard increase pattern that would work. For consistency during the experiments I adopted a standard width of fabric strip (one and one-half inches) which was the minimum needed for a consistent double-fold to hide the raw edges of the strip. The result was a standard increase that worked consistently, and made the development of fabric patterns an easy transition. The patterns in this of this book are all based on that standard width and increase, but if you want to use other widths or types of fabrics, see Chapter 15.

IF YOU ALREADY KNOW HOW TO CROCHET, READ THIS FIRST
I Mean It!

Millions of people know how to crochet and many have been crocheting with yarns for decades. If you're one of them, you are going to have trouble crocheting rag rugs simply because you are going to have to un-learn many of the habits you've acquired. The techniques for using fabric strip in crochet stitches are very different than what you've learned with yarn.

First, understand that fabric strip has a mind of its own. It will seek its "natural" stitch size no matter what size hook you use. You can make a crocheted rug with heavy wool fabric using the same hook as you would with a very light and narrow cotton strip. For years I used only a Boye, Size K metal hook for everything. The trick is to learn to let the fabric tell you how large the stitch should be, instead of expecting the hook to artificially control the size of the stitch.

Look at the various photographs of rugs-in-progress and notice that the crochet hook lies easily across the top of the work. With most fabric and hook combinations, you will need to pull up excess with each loop of the stitch to have the hook in that position. Whatever you do, don't work tightly. If you are an obsessively tight-crocheter, a very large hook can help (Q or above) but even then you may still be working too tightly. The test is that if you are struggling to make a stitch—you need to loosen up.

Fabric strip does not have the "give" that yarns do and it has a lot more body and friction. The stitches around the outside of a crocheted rug may appear to "stand up" from the surface instead of lying neatly along the edge. That appearance is caused by the way you hold the rug as you work and friction between the fabrics from one row to the next. Don't be alarmed if you notice that look. Lay the rug face down and pat or stroke the stitches into position. Alternately, you can roll up the rug (right side out) and the recent stitches will find where they are supposed to be. Slick fabrics will show this tendency the least and rough fabrics, the most.

The stitches used with rug making are the same as with "regular" crochet, so you don't have to know anything more than how to make a chain stitch, single crochet stitch and slip stitch to make the rugs shown. If you are a beginning crocheter, you can make rugs with only those most basic skills.

Learning to Crochet a High Quality Rug

There are a lot of crocheted rugs around today, but most of them are not quality rugs. Indications that a rug is poorly made include a loose structure, an open center, an irregular shape and a rough surface. Too many of the rugs being sold today at craft fairs are poor-quality rugs and they have turned many people away from the idea of crocheted rag rugs. If you pick up one of those rugs and your fingers go right through the surface holes, know that you're holding a doily, not a rug.

By contrast a well made crocheted or fabric tapestry has a tight, even center, a smooth, tight surface and a regular shape. It feels heavy for its size and appears solid and sturdy. Look at the rugs in this book and you will notice that there aren't holes or gaps in the surface. The surface stitches are so even that the designs nearly appear to be beaded rather than crocheted. (One husband visiting our rug shop confidently told his wife, "They have a machine in the back room to make them.") Of course, that wasn't true, but his impression that the rugs were so uniform, they were machine-made is the hallmark of a well made crocheted rug. That is the type of rug anyone can make—with the right directions.

CHAPTER 1

THE BASICS

Through this book, the term "standard crochet" is used for rugs made with a regular pattern of single crochet stitches using a single strand. Since these rugs are easily adapted to the fabric tapestry technique, they are presented together. (Once you learn to make a round "standard crochet" rug, it is easy to adapt to a round "fabric tapestry" rug.)

The term "fabric tapestry" signifies a rug made using two or more fabric strips at the same time to form a pattern in the rug. The beginner and novice patterns in this book require the use of only two strands at the same time. Throughout the book, I encourage the rug maker to use charted patterns in making their rugs. Once you are familiar with the charts, feel free to adapt the pattern for your own rug.

Fabric tapestry rugs are one of the most exciting rag rugs for the home crafter. They can be made in an almost limitless variety of patterns to accent any home. The technique of making fabric tapestry rugs is not difficult **if** you take the time to understand the "standard crochet" pattern **first**.

Fabric tapestry rugs do take a bit longer to complete than crocheted rugs, especially in the elaborate multi-strand patterns. Simple, two-strand designs require only about 10% more time and material to complete than a similar size crocheted rug.

Tools and Equipment

All you really need to crochet a rag rug is some fabric strip and a crochet hook. The size of the hook depends on two things:

1. The throat of the hook must large enough to grab the fabric strip securely (avoid hooks with a slit style throat); and

2. The hook should be comfortable in the rug maker's hand.

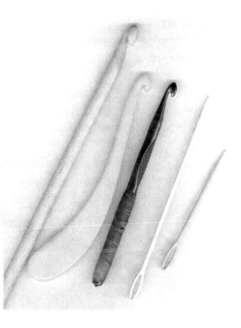

A standard metal crochet hook (Size K, L or larger) is fine or you can use the traditional wooden 10-inch hook (same sizes). The extra length in the wooden handle makes it easiest to use, but if you cannot find a wooden hook use metal or a sturdy plastic hook. Modern hooks with larger handles are a great innovation for rug makers and they really do reduce hand strain.

One common mistake in making crocheted rugs is to use a hook that is too large. Fabric strip will generate its own stitch size, and if you use too large a hook you will end up with a very loose rug structure, instead of the even surface that is desirable. It is best to use the smallest possible hook that will grab the fabric strip. I have used a size K (Boyes) hook for all weights of fabric strip from very light synthetics to very heavy woolens. An L hook is a good choice for just about any fabric. If you tend to crochet very tightly and are working with medium weight cottons should you use a size Q hook.

Other tools that you'll want to have on hand for crocheting rugs include:
A **sharp** pair of sewing scissors or a rotary cutter and mat for cutting fabric strips;
A lacing needle with an eye large enough to accept fabric strip;
Safety pins for marking stitch placement;
A sewing machine to join the fabric strips into one continuous strip;
Bias tape folders (if you are using traditional cotton fabrics) to fold the strip to hide the raw edges. See the Handbook Section for more information about techniques for double-folding fabric.

The Crochet Stitches
You only need a very basic knowlege of crochet to be able to make rugs. There are only three stitches used.

Chain stitch (used at the very beginning in the center of a rug)
Single crochet stitch (used for the body of the rug)
Slip stitch (used for the last few stitches at the outside edge of a rug)

To begin a rug using the chain stitch, made a slip knot in the end of the fabric strip, leaving a tail of four or five inches beyond the knot.

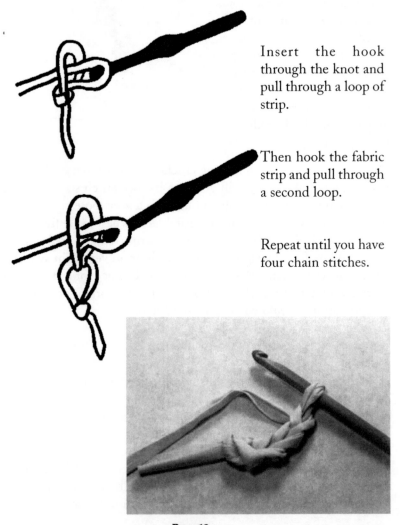

Insert the hook through the knot and pull through a loop of strip.

Then hook the fabric strip and pull through a second loop.

Repeat until you have four chain stitches.

The chain stitches are joined to a circle by pulling a loop through the original slip knot and the loop on the hook. Then two more chain stitches are made.

The single crochet stitches are made by inserting the hook into the center of the circle of chain stitches, and pulling up a loop. There will be two loops on the hook.

Pull another of fabric strip through the two loops on the hook and you have completed the first single crochet stitch.

Keep your stitching relaxed. If you have a tendency to crochet very tightly, you are doubling the effort needed to crochet a rug. Remember that fabric strip will form a "natural" stitch size depending on its weight and stiffness.

All of the rug patterns in this book use 1.5-inch strips of cotton or cotton-blend fabric. Do not use other widths or types of fabrics unless you read the information in Chapter 15 about how to modify the patterns for other materials.

The fabric strips shown are all double-folded to hide the raw edges. This type of fabric preparation is optional, but is the key to a professional-looking rug. It really makes a tremendous difference in the appearance of the rug, so I do encourage you not to skip the folding step. Properly preparing the fabric strip is fully half of the work that goes into making a rug. (For more information about fabric preparation, see the Handbook in Part 2 of this book.)

To Double-fold Fabric Strip

Fold edges to center

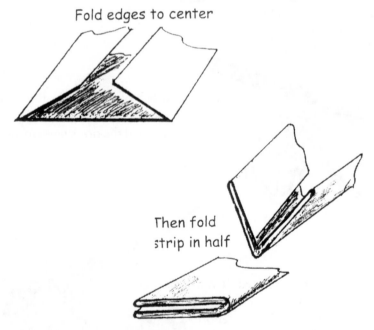

Then fold strip in half

Use a smooth finished fabric, if possible. Fabrics with rough textures have a lot of friction as the stitches are made. This makes extra work for you with each stitch. You may need to pre-wash heavily sized fabrics to make them easier to work.

CHAPTER 2

GETTING STARTED WITH A ROUND HOTPAD

A basic round hotpad is where to start with learning to crochet rugs. For the project you'll need about a yard and a half of 44-inch fabric cut into 1½-inch strips and joined together—about 35 yards of strip total. (The handbook section at the back of this book has all of the information about preparing your fabrics for a rug.) So, grab a hook and we'll get started.

Crocheted rugs are made using only the single crochet stitch in the body of the rug. A base of chain stitches is used to begin the rug and slip stitches are used to finish the edge. Since only these three stitches are used, I developed a system of "charting" the stitches to use as a visual reference. The charts eliminate the need for long written patterns and make it easy to develop a fabric tapestry design.

The symbols in the charts represent:

O — Chain Stitch

Q — One Single Crochet Stitch

W — A Pair of Single Crochet Stitches

◯ — Slip Stitch

For this first hotpad project, there is a photo, the chart and written directions in plain English (and in standard crochet notation) for each step along the way. But remember that crocheting with fabric is not the same as crocheting with yarn. While you work, focus on making each stitch large enough that the hook will lay easily across the top edge.

 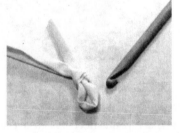

1. Make a slip knot at least two inches from the end of the fabric strip and insert the crochet hook into the loop.

2. Chain four stitches. Each stitch should be fairly loose. (CH 4)

3. With the fourth chain stitch still on the hook, insert the crochet hook into the original slip knot and pull a loop of fabric through the slip knot and the last chain stitch on the hook. (Join to circle.)

4. Chain two more stitches (CH 2)

5. Insert the crochet hook into the center of the circle formed by the chain stitches. Pull a ½- inch loop up through the center of the circle. You should have two loops on the hook. Pull a ½-inch loop of fabric through both loops on the hook. This completes the first single crochet stitch.

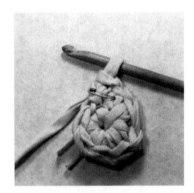

6. Repeat step 5 until seven single crochet stitches are inserted into the center of the circle. (SC 7 into center.)

7. Insert the crochet hook into the last chain stitch and make two single crochet stitches into it. Work under **both horizontal strands..** Mark this pair of stitches with a safety pin. (SC 2 in next 8.) Make two single crochet stitches in each stitch in the previous round. When you reach the tail of the chain stitch, pull it to tighten the center. Then work over the tail to hide it. You will have eight pairs of stitches counting the pair marked with the safety pin. There are sixteen stitches in this round altogether. This round should end up in the space just before the safety pin. (SC16, 2 SC in ea. previous.)

9. Insert a pair of single crochet stitches into the space between the pair of stitches marked with the safety pin. (2 SC in next sp.)

10. Make one single crochet stitch in the space between the pair marked with the safety pin and the next pair of stitches.

11. Continue around the row until you reach the marked pair, inserting a pair of single crochet stitches into the space inside each previous pair and making one single crochet stitch in the space between pairs. (SC 24, 2 SC into ea. prev. pair, 1 SC between pairs). You will have 24 stitches in this round, eight pairs of stitches and eight individual stitches, one between each pair.

12. Note that there are now spaces in between each pair of stitches that will accept two individual stitches.

Complete the next round by inserting a pair of single crochet stitches inside each pair in the previous round, and making one single crochet stitch into each of the two spaces between the pairs.
(SC 32, 2 SC into ea. prev. pair, SC in each space between pairs.)

13. Between each pair of stitches there are spaces to accommodate three individual stitches. Complete this round by inserting a pair of single

crochet stitches into each pair of the previous round, with each pair separated by three individual single crochet stitches.
(SC 40, 2 SC into ea. prev. pair, 1 SC into each space between pairs.)

For a simple round, finish with 3 slip stitches. For a larger hotpad with a hanger continue with directions 14-17.

14. For the last row around the edge of the hot pad, do not pair up the single crochet stitches as in the previous rounds. Insert one single crochet stitch into each space (SC 40) around the outside.

15 To make a loop to hang up the hot pad, chain seven stitches. (CH 7)

16. Insert the crochet hook into the next crochet stitch an pull the rest of the strip including the end up through the stitch and the loop on the hook.

17. Thread the end of the strip into the eye of a lacing needle and insert the needle into the back side of the next crochet stitch.

You should have enough strip left to stretch twice around the outside of the hot pad. (If not, skip this step and go to the next.) Using the lacing needle, insert a whip stitch into each space around the outside to create a more finished edge.

Lace the strip under several crochet stitches and sew it in place with a needle and thread. Clip off the excess strip.

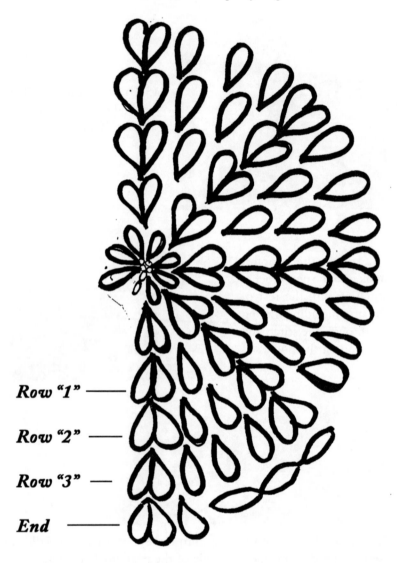

Row "1" ——

Row "2" ——

Row "3" ——

End ——

You will have noticed that the pairs in each row are lined up and each row has one more stitch in it than the row before. That pattern makes it easy to remember. It also allows for a shortcut in charting. The row with only one stitch between the pairs is called Row "1". The row with two stitches between pairs is called Row "2" and is followed by Row "3".

As the work progresses out from the center, the pairs of stitches are separated by one more individual single crochet stitch than the pairs in the previous row, so Row "3" will be followed by Row "4", then Row "5" and so on. This pattern of increase is the basis of all round crocheted work with fabric.

You may be tempted to go on to a larger project using this hotpad as the center of the rug. It isn't a good idea with your first hotpad, since your stitches will have gotten more consistent as you worked. If you are ready to go on, just pull the stitches out and start again so that the center of your rug will be as even as the rest of it.

You want your finished hotpad to have a tight, even center and a nice round shape. And, of course it should lay perfectly flat. With a hotpad like this, you're ready to begin making rugs.

Because it is so much easier to crochet rugs visually, take this opportunity to compare the standard written style of directions with the charted pattern opposite. In the charted pattern, the pairs of stitches are highlighted to help you count the individual stitches between rows.

8-INCH ROUND HOTPAD
Standard Written Crochet Directions

Beg at center with a slip knot, Ch 4, Sl St in first Ch to form ring. CORE: Ch 2, 7 Sc in ring, Do not chain up between rounds, Work proceeds in a spiral.

BASE: 2 Sc in each space around, working under both top strands. — 16 Sc

ROW '1': *2 Sc in next space, 1 Sc in next space, repeat from * around (eight repeats in all) —24 Sc

ROW '2': *2 Sc in next space, 1 Sc in next 2 spaces, repeat from * around (eight repeats in all) —32 Sc

ROW '3': *2 Sc in next space, 1 Sc in next 3 spaces, repeat from * around (eight repeats in all) —40 Sc

LAST ROUND: 1 Sc in each space around.

LOOP: CH 7, Join to next Sc with Sl St. End off. Lace end through stitches. Sew to secure.

ABBREVIATIONS:
Ch = Chain Stitch
Sc = Single Crochet Stitch
Sl St = Slip Stitch
Fm = From
Beg = Beginning

Charted Pattern for Round Hotpad
Notice how the paired stitches line up.

CHAPTER 3

CROCHETING ROUND RUGS

Once you've completed the first hotpad, you're ready to make a round or octagonal crocheted rag rug. The increase pattern is exactly the same with eight pairs of stitches in each round. With small projects, the round shape only needs a final row of crocheting that is made without any paired stitches.

Because I always encourage beginning with small projects, the first is a 15-inch chairpad, made of a single color. It is shown above with another beginner project, a small oval rug made in the same fabric. (See the chapter on oval rugs.)

For the chairpad, you will need 4-3/4 yards of fabric, cut into 1-1/2-inch strips. That is about 133 yards of strip. On the facing page is the charted pattern for the chairpad. Note that it is just like the hotpad in the previous chapter, except that it continues through Row "8" before the final row is crocheted.

Refer to the step-by-step directions to help you get started, and if you have a busy print on your fabric, use safety pins to mark the position of each pair of stitches.

Use the same fabric strip to make the ties for the chair back.

15-Inch Round Chairpad: Charted Pattern

1
2
3
4
5
6
7
-8
END

Making Larger Rugs

If you continue to line up the paired stitches, a round rugs will begin to take on an octagonal shape. There is nothing wrong with an octagonal rug, but if you want a round shape, adjustments need to be made to the basic pattern.

For the first eight rounds, the paired stitches are lined up—just like in the hotpad project. For an octagonal rug, the pairs continue to be lined up in every row, but for a round rug, the pairs will be moved three spaces from the pair in the previous round. Until you have some practice with the method, it is a good idea to mark each pair of stitches with a safety pin.

The patterns in this chapter are for fairly small rugs to get you started, but the octagonal and round patterns can be extended to as large as you want to handle. You will want to know about how much fabric to have on hand for other sizes of rugs and the chart below can be used as a guide. (See the handbook section for more information about estimating fabric consumption.)

Rug Diameter (in inches)	Yards of 45-inch fabric
24"	9
30"	15-1/2
36"	21
42"	28
48"	36
54"	46
60"	55
66"	68
72"	80

I know these numbers look like a lot of fabric, but you'll be surprised how much you'll be able to find in your sewing cupboard, or yardages at yard sales. Also, watch for sales on sheets. One twin flat sheet is roughly the equivalent of four yards of 45-inch fabric. And, remember that these rugs will last a very long time.

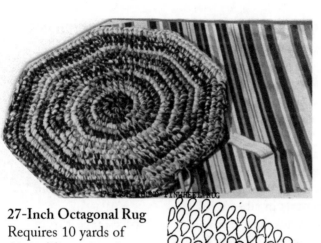

27-Inch Octagonal Rug

Requires 10 yards of fabric .The pairs of stitches are highlited in the charted pattern. The rug in the photo was made using a striped fabric which results in a traditional look of hit-or-miss, but by using a decorator fabric the colors are coordinated.

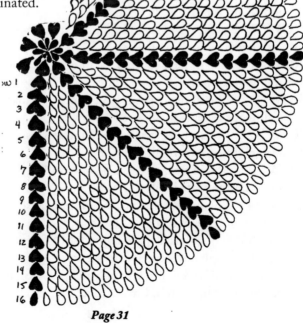

27-INCH OCTAGONAL RUG: WRITTEN DIRECTIONS

(Corresponds to charted pattern on previous page.)

Beg at center, Ch 4, Sl St in first Ch to form ring.

CORE: Ch 2, 7 Sc in ring, Do not chain up between rounds, Work proceeds in a spiral.

BASE: 2 Sc in each space around, working under both top strands. —16 Sc

ROW '1': *2 Sc in next space, 1 Sc in next space, repeat from * around (eight repeats in all —24 Sc

ROW '2': *2 Sc in next space, 1 Sc in next 2 spaces, repeat from * around (eight repeats in all —32 Sc

ROW '3': *2 Sc in next space, 1 Sc in next 3 spaces, repeat from * around (eight repeats in all —40 Sc

ROW '4': *2 Sc in next space, 1 Sc in next 4 spaces, repeat from * around (eight repeats in all —48 Sc

ROW '5': *2 Sc in next space, 1 Sc in next 5 spaces, repeat from * around (eight repeats in all —56 Sc

ROW '6': *2 Sc in next space, 1 Sc in next 6 spaces, repeat from * around (eight repeats in all —64 Sc

ROW '7': *2 Sc in next space, 1 Sc in next 7 spaces, repeat from * around (eight repeats in all —72 Sc

ROW '8': *2 Sc in next space, 1 Sc in next 8 spaces, repeat from * around (eight repeats in all —80 Sc

ROW '9': *2 Sc in next space, 1 Sc in next 9 spaces, repeat from * around (eight repeats in all —88 Sc

ROW '10': *2 Sc in next space, 1 Sc in next 10 spaces, repeat from * around (eight repeats in all —96 Sc

ROW '11': *2 Sc in next space, 1 Sc in next 11 spaces, repeat from * around (eight repeats in all —104 Sc

ROW '12': *2 Sc in next space, 1 Sc in next 12 spaces, repeat from * around (eight repeats in all —112 Sc

ROW '13': *2 Sc in next space, 1 Sc in next 13 spaces, repeat from * around (eight repeats in all —120 Sc

ROW '14': *2 Sc in next space, 1 Sc in next 14 spaces, repeat from * around (eight repeats in all —128 Sc

LAST ROW: Sc in each space around, Sl St in next 3 Sc. End off. Lace end through stitches. Sew to secure.

ABBREVIATIONS: Ch = Chain Stitch, Sc = Single Crochet Stitch. Sl St = Slip Stitch, Fm = From

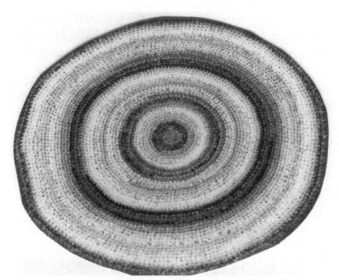

MAKING A ROUND RUG

Converting the basic octagonal pattern to make a true round rug is fairly simple to do. Look at the charted patterns for each shape. Both shapes are identical having the pairs of stitches lined up through Row "8" (where there are eight single stitches between each pair of stitches).

For a true round rug, beginning at Row "9" the paired stitches in each row are shifted three spaces further along than the pair in the previous row. This progression can be continued to any size. Until you have practice with the method, mark each pair with a safety pin to remind yourself of the placement of the paired stitches.

Begin your rug by following the directions for the round hotpad in the previous chapter through row "3." Then, make rows "4" through "8" in the same fashion, keeping the paired stitches lined up. Beginning at row "9" mark each pair with a safety pin.

Make one single crochet stitch in the pair of the previous row and three more stitches (one in each space). Then insert two stitches in the next space. Move the safety pin from the previous row to this pair of stitches. Continue around the row, insert a pair three spaces after the pair in the previous row and move the safety pin you just passed to mark the new pair.

As long as each new pair gets marked with the safety pin, you really don't even have to count stitches from here on out. Just insert a pair three spaces after each safety pin and you'll have the right stitch pattern.

However large you make your rug, remember to make the last row without any pairs for a nice even edge.

BASIC ROUND PATTERN FOR CROCHETED RUGS

(Corresponds to charted pattern on following page.)

Chain 4, join to ring.

CORE: Ch 2, 7 Sc in ring, Do not chain up between rounds, Work proceeds in a spiral.

BASE: 2 Sc in each space around, working under both top strands. —16 Sc

ROW '1': *2 Sc in next space, 1 Sc in next space, repeat from * around (eight repeats in all —24 Sc

ROW '2': *2 Sc in next space, 1 Sc in next 2 spaces, repeat from * around (eight repeats in all —32 Sc

ROW '3': *2 Sc in next space, 1 Sc in next 3 spaces, repeat from * around (eight repeats in all —40 Sc

ROW '4': *2 Sc in next space, 1 Sc in next 4 spaces, repeat from * around (eight repeats in all —48 Sc

ROW '5': *2 Sc in next space, 1 Sc in next 5 spaces, repeat from * around (eight repeats in all —56 Sc

ROW '6': *2 Sc in next space, 1 Sc in next 6 spaces, repeat from * around (eight repeats in all —64 Sc

ROW '7': *2 Sc in next space, 1 Sc in next 7 spaces, repeat from * around (eight repeats in all —72 Sc

ROW '8': *2 Sc in next space, 1 Sc in next 8 spaces, repeat from * around (eight repeats in all —80 Sc

FURTHER ROUNDS: Proceed as follows—Sc into any paired stitches in the previous round, 1 Sc in each of the next 3 spaces, 2 Sc in next space, 1 Sc in all following spaces until next pair is reached.

END: Sc in each space around, Sl St in next 3 spaces under the back strand only. End off. Lace end of strip through stitches, sew to secure it, and clip off any excess. (You can also make a finished edge of whip stitching. See the directions for project 2.)

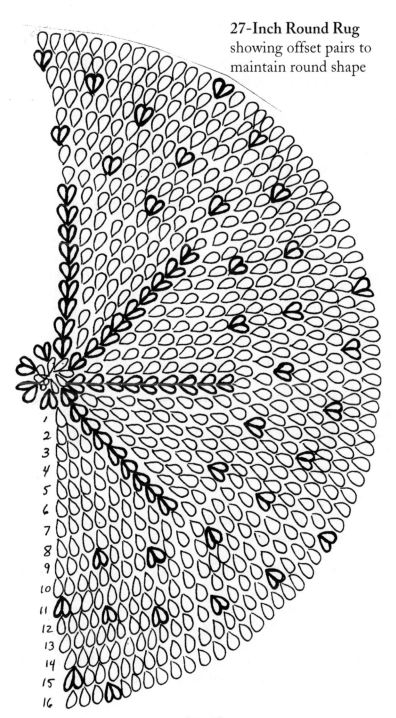

27-Inch Round Rug
showing offset pairs to
maintain round shape

1
2
3
4
5
6
7
8
9
10
11
12
13
14
15
16

Making Very Large Round or Octagonal Rugs

Following the basic patterns, you can crochet a round or octagonal rug of any size. However, large rugs get to be very heavy and as you stitch, you'll be constantly moving that weight as you work around the outside. This can put a lot of strain on your neck and shoulders and I developed a pinched nerve from doing just that. So, if you plan on a large rug, find a table to lay the rug across, and a chair on casters that will let you move around the rug without having to lift it repeatedly.

When rugs get to be three or four across, some people notice that the rug begins to "full up" or wave. This is caused by the cumulative effect of many rows of stitches were made just a little bit too tightly for the fabric being used. (I know that sounds backwards, but that's what causes it.) If your rug does start to wave, make a complete round without any pairs and then resume the pairs in the next row. You don't have to pull out any rounds as long as you catch the wave just as it is starting to form.

Traditional Designs in Standard Crocheted Rugs

Standard crocheted rugs were often made of cast off clothing, but that didn't mean that they were boring. Often, the old fabrics were dyed to specific color schemes so that they would fit a particular design. The most common patterns in these old rugs were, hit-or-miss, wide bands and single- or double-spirals.

All of these traditional patterns can be combined in a rug. For example, a wide band pattern in which one band is a spiral (see charted pattern) or with alternating bands of hit-or-miss.

The name "hit-or-miss" is really misleading, because the best of these rugs were really not put together just any old way. Instead the colors were sorted by shades so that a subtle progression of colors and shades flowed from the center to the edge of the rug.

Black borders were also commonly used in old rugs, but that makes the rug look smaller, so dark borders should be used cautiously.

27-inch "Hit-or-Miss"
showing a progression of six colors

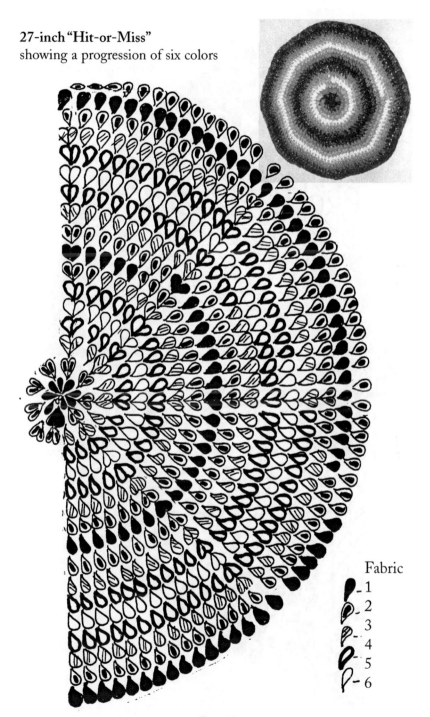

Fabric
- 1
- 2
- 3
- 4
- 5
- 6

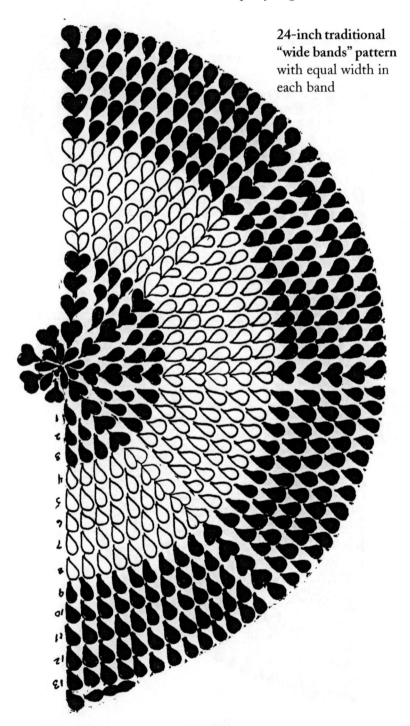

24-inch traditional "wide bands" pattern with equal width in each band

Single- and Double-Spiral Rugs

A spiral rug is a delightful variation of the standard crocheted rug, and can be made in any size. The tricky part of a spiral is just at the beginning. For a single-spiral, you will add in a second color (wherever you want) and then crochet with the two alternately. Just work each row around until you "catch up" to the other color. Then crochet with the second color.

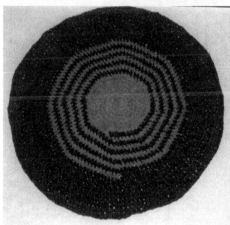

To add a second fabric, just pull a loop through any stitch, and then single crochet in the next space. When you are ready to end the spiral, simply make two slip stitches and end off by pulling then fabric strip up through the last stitch.

Double-spirals are only slightly more complicated. Two fabrics are added at opposite sides of the rug on the same row. Then the three fabrics are crocheted in order. You'll be working with each color in sequence, and all you have to remember is to always make a pair of stitches inside each previous pair.

38-inch Single Spiral Rug
see photo on previous page

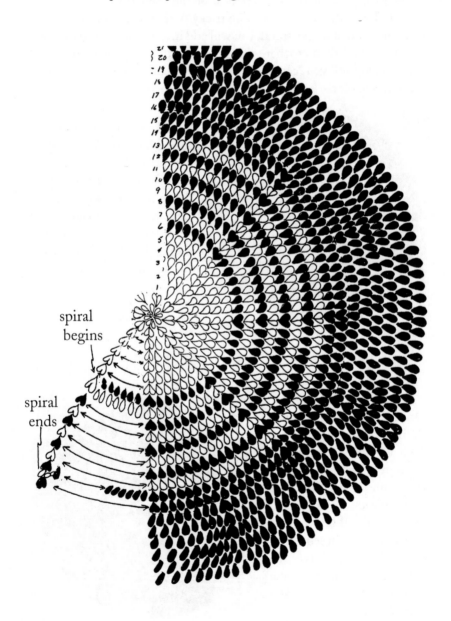

spiral
begins

spiral
ends

27-inch Double-spiral Rug
Spiral begins on Row "1"

CHAPTER 4

ROUND FABRIC TAPESTRY RUGS

Fabric tapestry rugs look very complex, but they are really a logical step from standard crochet. "Tapestry crochet" is simply the process of using two or more strands at the same time. You crochet with one strand and cover up the other(s) as you stitch. This allows you to change the color that shows on the surface of the rug, creating any design you desire. If you've completed a round crocheted hotpad, you're ready to tackle the next step working with two strands of fabric.

Making fabric tapestry rugs is so much easier when you are comfortable with the charted patterns. In fact, once most people become familiar with charted patterns, they are able to look at a fabric tapestry rug and follow the design from the rug itself.

Basic Fabric Tapestry Technique
Begin the center of your hotpad or rug with just one strand of fabric strip. Once the very center is formed (the row which is worked into the circle of chain stitches) you can add your second fabric at any point. Most of the beginner "pinwheel" patterns require adding the second strip at the beginning of Row "1." (See the charted pattern.)

You can begin the second strip of fabric at any point. In this series of photos the second strip is being added at the beginning of row "1" (where there is one single crochet stitch separating each Pair). Following the sequence here you can add colors, or change colors at any time as you work on a rug or other project.

To Change Colors

1. Begin by drawing up a loop of the new color of fabric strip. There will be one loop of the old color on the hook.

2. Draw a second loop of the new fabric through both loops on the hook. This completes the first single crochet sitch with the new fabric.

3. Sew the end of the new fabric strip to the top edge of the previous round of stitches.

4. Begin crocheting with the new color, enclosing the old color inside each stitch. **Note that the strip to be enclosed should be held to the front side of the work, and the strip you are using to crochet should be held to the back.**

5. To change back to the original color, just reverse the positions of the two strips of fabric and start crocheting with the first color. For fabric tapestry designs that have more than two colors in a round, the process is the same. The strip that is used for crocheting is held to the back, and the strips that are being carried along are held to the front side.

The simplest patterns in fabric tapestry are based on the paired stitches. Below is the same charted pattern as for the crocheted hotpad but with the paired stitches darkened. If you look at the chart, you can see that beginning with row "1" a lighter fabric is added and the dark fabric is used only for the paired stitches.

All of the patterns which use the paired stitches the key part of the design, are called "Pinwheel" patterns. The simplest of which are made by using one color of fabric just for the center and paired stitches.

At the left is the center of a rug showing the basic pinwheel patten. If it looks familiar, it is. In the "Getting Started" chapter, the hotpad chart is shown with the pairs highlighted. That same pattern, you can revisit to make a pinwheel pattern hotpad (which is an excellent first project for learning fabric tapestry).

If you want to make a larger pinwheel rug, the lines of the paired stitches are continued. In the previous chapter on round standard crocheted rugs, the pattern with highlighted pairs can also be used for a fabric tapestry "pinwheel" rug.

Notice that there is a difference between the charted patterns which show the paired stitches in fairly straight lines, and the rugs themselves. The paired stitches will form a slight counter-clockwise curve. That is just part of how crochet works and can be put to good use for adding interest to your own rug designs.

All of the following patterns in this chapter are variations on the basic pinwheel. Feel free to experiment with the patterns, adding or subtracting lines or rows of different colors.

A "Tiffany" Rug or Chairpad

The "tiffany" variation of a pinwheel pattern simply adds rows of the same dark color used to highlight the paired stitches. As the rug gets larger, the dark rows are increased and the stitches next to the pairs are also made with dark strip.

The most effective use of the tiffany pattern is to use a different shading for each of the lighter bands of color. The rug give the effect of stained glass

Chart for 35-inch Tiffany Rug
(for the chairpad, stop at row "12".

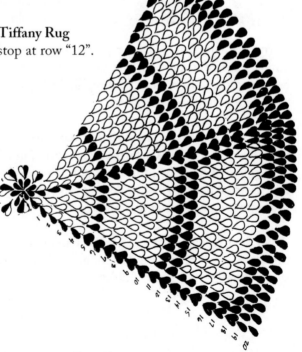

The "Rolling Wheel" variation

36-inch rug using 14.5 yards light fabric, 6 yards dark fabric

In the Rolling Wheel, the pairs are made in contrasting fabric, just like a regular pinwheel. However, each pair is shifted by one space to emphasize the curve. Beginning at Row "1" insert each pair in the space directly after the pair in the previous row.

The "Graded" Pinwheel

In this variation, there is a gradual color change in both the arms of the pinwheel and the background fabric. The chart shows a dark to light sequence and the rug a light to dark progression. (27-inch rug using 7.5 yards dark, 3.8 yards medium, 2.5 yards light)

Graded Pinwheel Charted Pattern

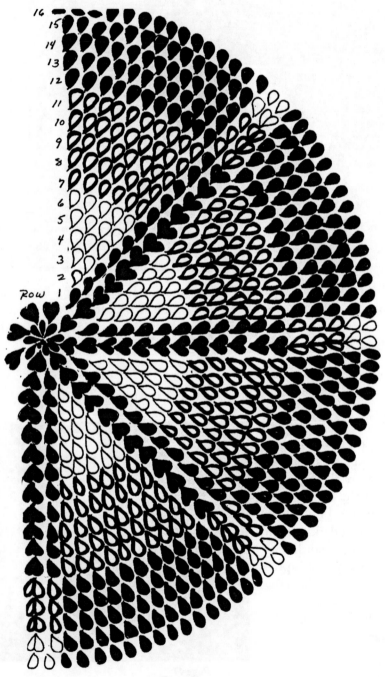

Windmill Blades

This pinwheel variation changes colors in the middle of each pair and in the middle of each section, creating the effect of whirling blades. (24-inch rug using 5 yards light, 6 yards dark fabric.)

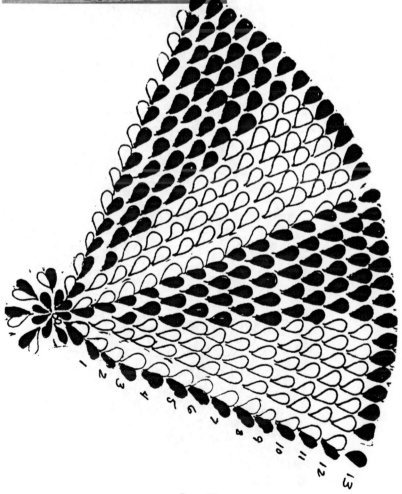

Variying the ends of a pinwheel

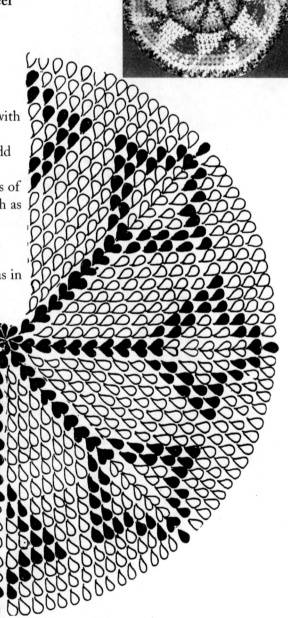

If you get bored with a plain pinwheel design, you can add other figures or shapes to the ends of the pinwheel, such as the "tulips" in the chart below. The figures do not all have to be alike, as in the photo.

More Pinwheel Variations

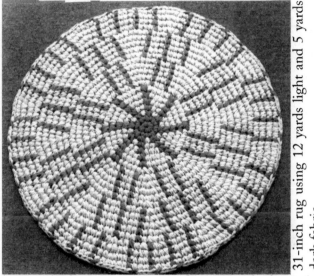

31-inch rug using 12 yards light and 5 yards dark fabric

In the rug above, only the very center is made as a standard pinwheel. Then the pairs are not highlighted. Instead, stripes are created of individual stitches between the pairs.

24-inch rug using 8 yards light and 4 yards dark fabric

If you look closely at this photography, you should be able to spot the lines of the paired stitches made in the lighter fabric (they are the continuous light lines). The arms of the pinwheel are made wider with an extra stitch of light fabric. Then stripes are created with two stitches of darker fabric.

On the first page of this chapter is a photograph of a round rug, which looks very complicated. If you look closely at it, you should be able to spot the "pinwheel" lines formed by the paired stitches. In each row, the color is changed with every stitch creating "V" shaped accents all around the rug. Below is the charted pattern for that rug, which I called "layers of pinwheels" but probably deserves a fancier name. That rug was 30 inches across and used 8 yards of dark fabric and 7 yards of light fabric.

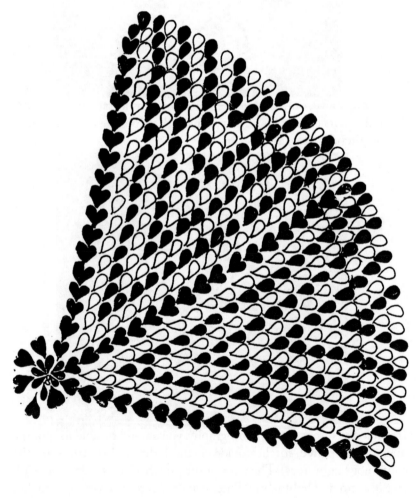

CHAPTER 5

CROCHETING OVAL RUGS

Once you have mastered the basics of the round shape, you will be ready to move on to oval rugs. And understanding how the round and oval shapes are related makes it easier to follow the patterns for oval rugs.

In essence, if you cut a round rug in half, and separate the halves with a section of straight stitching, you have created an oval rug.

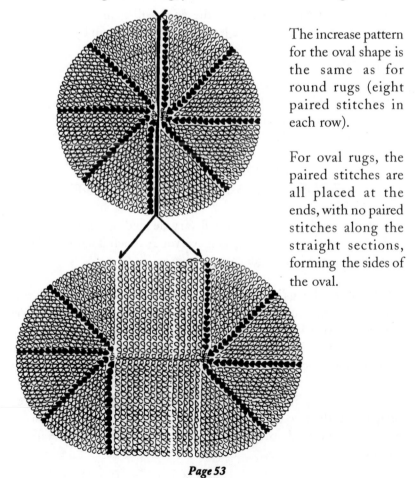

The increase pattern for the oval shape is the same as for round rugs (eight paired stitches in each row).

For oval rugs, the paired stitches are all placed at the ends, with no paired stitches along the straight sections, forming the sides of the oval.

Determining the Size of Oval Rugs

Oval rugs can be made in any size from long and narrow to short and broad. The dimensions of the finished rug are determined by the length of the base chain at the beginning of the rug. Find this length by subtracting the width from the length of the size rug you want. For example, if you want to make a rug that is 5 feet long and 3 feet wide, you will need a base chain that is 2 feet long (5 - 3 =2). As a general rule of thumb (when using cotton fabrics) 10 stitches in the chain will add six inches in length to the rug overall, so a 3' X 5' oval would begin with a base chain of 40 stitches.

For ovals over three feet wide, the ends will gain in length at an increased rate, so decrease the length of the base chain by about 10%.

Most of the rug patterns that follow are for ovals that are two feet wide and three feet long. Those will require **12 yards** of 44-45 inch fabric. If you wish to make oval rugs in a size not shown in the projects here, you can estimate the fabric yardage (for cottons) needed with the following formula:

LENGTH X WIDTH X 2 =
YARDS OF 44-45-INCH FABRIC NEEDED

The actual yardage consumed will vary depending on the type and weight of fabric you are using, and everyone's touch is a little different so use this formula as a generous estimate.

Oval crocheted rugs can be made in many surface designs. Narrow bands of color, hit-or-miss, color progressions, wide bands and dappled patterns all work well in the oval shape. Before you begin any oval rug project, make a practice oval piece so that you understand the construction process and can follow the charted patterns more easily.

The step-by-step instructions are for using a single color to make a sample oval the size of a stair runner. For the practice piece, you will need about **60 yards** of prepared fabric strip (about 2-1/4 yards of fabric).

Step-by-Step: Beginning an Oval Crocheted Rug
with photos and corresponding charted pattern

1. Make a slip knot in the end of the rug strip and insert the crochet hook. Leave at least three inches of strip off the end of the knot.

2. Chain 12 stitches (or more for a longer rug), each 10 stitches in the base chain adds about six inches to the length of the rug. Mark the chain on the hook with a safety pin.

3. Chain two more stitches.

4. Insert the hook into the chain marked with the safety pin, and make one single crochet stitch.

5. Insert one single crochet stitch into each chain (Sc 12 in all) until the original slip knot is reached.

6. Insert FOUR single crochet stitches into the original slip knot (Sc 4) to "turn the corner" around the end of the chain. Pull up on the end of the strip forming the slip knot to tighten it, and sew the end securely to the edge of the chain stitches.

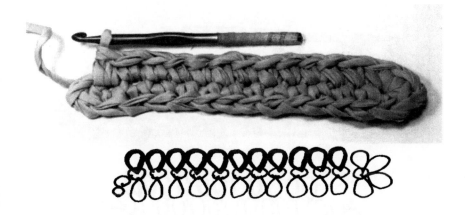

7. Insert one single crochet stitch in each chain stitch, exactly opposite the other single crochet stitches and in the same holes as the other side's stitches were made. (Sc 12)

8. Insert FOUR single crochet stitches into the next chain stitch. This will "turn the corner" at this end of the rug and complete the "Core" row.

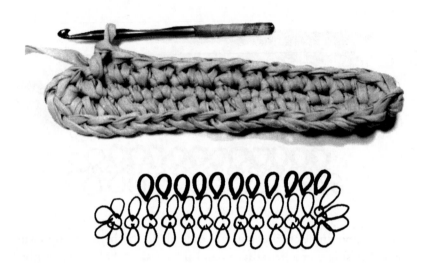

9. Insert one single crochet stitch into each of the next 12 spaces (Sc 12). Now you are ready to "turn the corner" again.

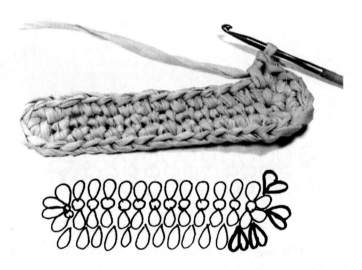

10. Make a pair of single crochet stitches into EACH OF THE NEXT FOUR SPACES. (2 Sc in each of next 4 spaces)

11. Single crochet along the side (Sc 12) with one stitch in each space to reach the other end.

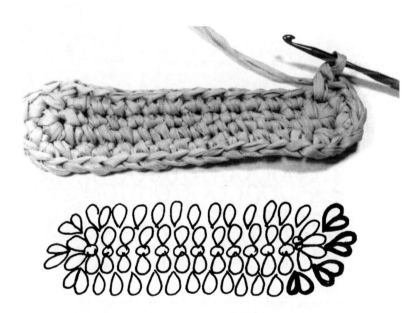

12. Insert a PAIR of single crochet stitches into each of the next four spaces. (2 Sc in each of next 4 spaces). This completes the "Base" row.

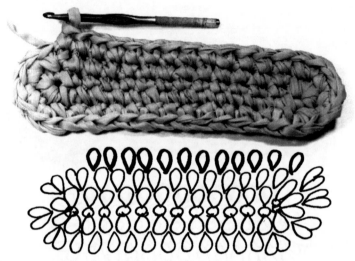

13. Single crochet along the side (Sc 13) with one stitch in each space until the first pair at the far end is reached.

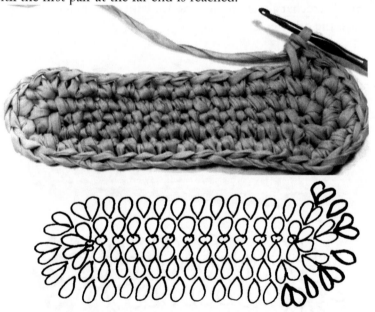

14. Insert a pair of single crochet stitches into the next space, then one single crochet stitch in the following space (between the pairs). Repeat this four times. (Note that the pairs of stitches you make in this row line up with the pairs of stitches in the previous row.) *2 Sc in next space, 1 Sc in next space, repeat fm* four times total.

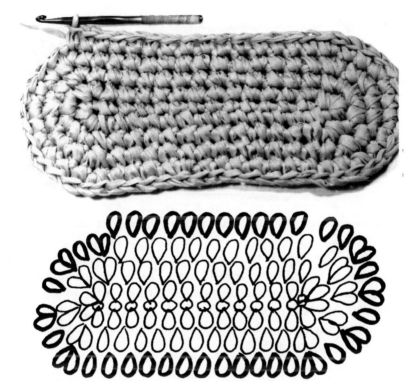

15. Repeat instruction #13, and #14. (They are each repeated only once, then proceed to #16). This will complete Row '1'.

16. Insert a pair of single crochet stitches into the next space, then one single crochet stitch in to each of the following two spaces. Note that the pairs of stitches in this row of stitches in this row line up with the pairs of stitches in the previous row. Continue around the corner, with each pair of stitches separated by two individual stitches. (*2 Sc in next space, 1 Sc in each of next two spaces, Repeat from* four times). Then Single crochet along the edge until you reach the next pair of stitches. (Note how this corresponds to Row "2" in the round shape.)

17. Complete the next end and side by repeating instruction #16.

(Note that the ends of the oval at this point are completed to the equivalent of Row '2' in the round shape. That is, each pair of stitches is separated by two individual stitches. Just like in the round shape Row '2' is followed by Row '3', then Row '4' and so on, with the row number signifying how many individual single crochet stitches are placed between the pairs.)

18. (Optional) To finish the stairpad, crochet one more row all of the way around without using any paired stitches. (The final row of any oval project is made without any pairs.)

FINISHING OFF AN OVAL RUG

Just like in the round shape, there are no paired stitches on the final outside row of an oval rug. Just single crochet around, until you are at the curve on the end, in about the position shown in the photo.

Ending off an oval rug is always done along the curve at the end of the rug, where it is least conspicuous. Complete three slip stitches, through the back thread only. Then pull up the end of the rug strip. Lace the end through several of the stitches in the last row. Sew the end in place and clip off the excess. (You can also do a finished edge with a whip stitch around the rug.)

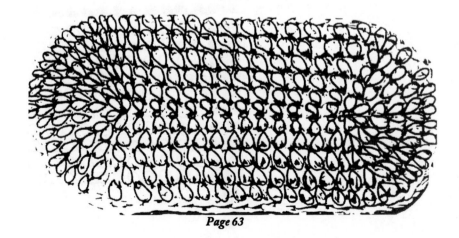

Continuing with the Oval Pattern

Small oval rugs can be completed by continuing to line up the paired stitches at each end, but eventually the lines of paired stitches will form pointy spots on the end of the rug (just like an octagonal rug).

The charted pattern below will make an oval 18 inches wide and 27 inches long, which is a good size for a first rug. (Allow 8 to 9 yards of fabric for the rug.) See the photo at the beginning of Chapter 2.

It is begun with a base of 11 chain stitches so you can follow the step by step directions to get the rug started and then follow the chart. (The center stitches and paired stitches are highlighted.)

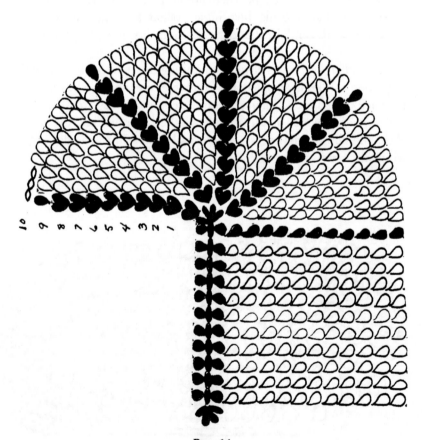

Rounding the Ends of an Oval Rug

To maintain a rounded end in larger ovals, it is necessary to begin shifting the paired stitches, exactly like in the round shape. The pairs are shifted beginning at Row '9' so that the curve on the ends is maintained.

The charted pattern below is for an oval 36 inches long and 24 inches wide. It is begun with a base chain of 19-20 stitches. (Allow 12 to 13 yards of fabric for an oval this size.)

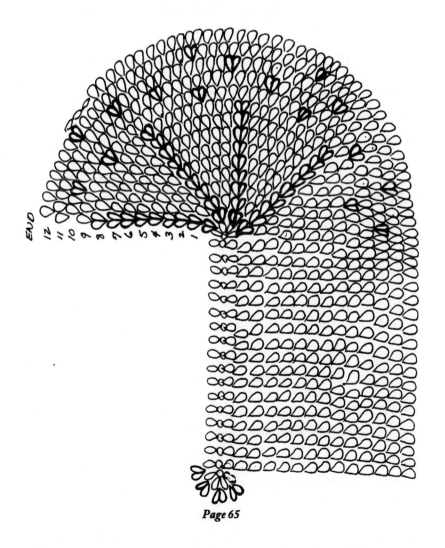

BASIC OVAL PATTERN: 24" x 36" RUG
Using written crochet directions.
(Use either these written directions or the chart. They are confusing if you try to follow both at the same time.)

Uses 12 to 13 yards of fabric, cut into 1-1/2 inch strip.

Begin with Slip Knot, Chain 17, mark chain on hook with safety pin, Chain 2
CORE: Place hook into chain marked with pin to start. Sc 17, 4 Sc into slip knot (pull end of strip to tighten and sew in place). Sc 17, 4 Sc in last chain stitch

BASE: *Sc 17, 2 Sc in each of the next 4 spaces, repeat from*

ROW '1': *Sc 18, Alternate 2 Sc and 1 Sc in each of next 8 spaces, repeat from*

ROW '2': * Sc 19, [2 Sc in next space, 1 Sc in each of next 2 spaces], Repeat [ ] 4 times in all, then repeat from*

ROW '3': * Sc 20, [2 Sc in next space, 1 Sc in each of next 3 spaces], Repeat [ ] 4 times in all, then repeat from*

ROW '4': * Sc 21, [2 Sc in next space, 1 Sc in each of next 4 spaces], Repeat [ ] 4 times in all, then repeat from*

ROW '5': * Sc 22, [2 Sc in next space, 1 Sc in each of next 5 spaces], Repeat [ ] 4 times in all, then repeat from*

ROW '6': * Sc 23, [2 Sc in next space, 1 Sc in each of next 6 spaces], Repeat [ ] 4 times in all, then repeat from*

ROW '7': * Sc 24, [2 Sc in next space, 1 Sc in each of next 7 spaces], Repeat [ ] 4 times in all, then repeat from*

ROW '8': * Sc 25, [2 Sc in next space, 1 Sc in each of next 8 spaces], Repeat [ ] 4 times in all, then repeat from*

ROW '9': * Sc 20, 2 Sc in next space, 1 Sc in next 9 spaces, 2 Sc in next space, 1 Sc in next 9 spaces, 2 Sc in next space, 1 Sc in next 9 spaces, 2 Sc in next space, 1 Sc in next 6 spaces, Repeat from*

ROW '10': * Sc 25, 2 Sc in next space, 1 Sc in next 10 spaces, 2 Sc in next space, 1 Sc in next 10 spaces, 2 Sc in next space, 1 Sc in next 10 spaces, 2 Sc in next space, 1 Sc in next 2 spaces, Repeat from*

ROW '11': * Sc 19, 2 Sc in next space, 1 Sc in next 11 spaces, 2 Sc in next space, 1 Sc in next 11 spaces, 2 Sc in next space, 1 Sc in next 11 spaces, 2 Sc in next space, 1 Sc in next 11 spaces, Repeat from*

ROW '12': * Sc 24, 2 Sc in next space, 1 Sc in next 12 spaces, 2 Sc in next space, 1 Sc in next 12 spaces, 2 Sc in next space, 1 Sc in next 12 spaces, 2 Sc in next space, 1 Sc in next 7 spaces, Repeat from*

END: Sc around with one stitch in each space, ending along curve. Sl st in 3 spaces, end off. Lace end of strip through stitches. Sew to secure.

FOR LARGER OVAL RUGS
Rows follow in numerical order (Row '13', '14', '15', etc) just like in the round shape. Four pairs of single crochet stitches are made at each end of the rug on each round.

The paired stitches are placed 3 spaces beyond the pair in the previous row generally. Note that no pairs are placed beyond the line formed by the fourth pair of stitches in Rows '1' through '8'. Instead, move the first pair of the next row back to the beginning of the curve, and do the correct count for the next row to place the other three pairs in the row.

If the ends of the oval begin to "full up" or wave, crochet one full round without any paired stitches and then resume with four pairs of stitches at each end. You do not need to pull out the previous stitches as long as the wave has not become too pronounced.

An oval rug should always be ended along a curved edge. End with three slip stitches. (See step by step directions for ending an oval.)

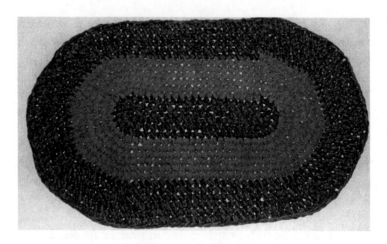

24" x 36" OVAL, WIDE BAND RUG

Select medium weight cottons or cotton blend fabrics (calico, broadcloth, etc.) To make the rug shown in the photograph you will need 1-1/2 yards of fabric for the center; 4-1/2 yards for the middle band, and 6-1/2 yards of fabric for the outer band. Cut strips 1-1/2 inches wide.

DIRECTIONS:
FOLLOW THE CHARTED PATTERN OR THE WRITTEN DIRECTIONS FOR THE OVAL RUG.

1. Complete the "Base" row, the "Core" row and Row '1' with the first fabric.

2. Change to the second color, and complete Rows '2' through '7' using the second fabric.

3. Change to the last color, and complete Row '8' through "End" with it.

Suggestions and Variations for Wide Band Rugs

If you are using three different fabrics with different colors and tones, use the middle tone for the center band. A very light tone in the center will seem to jump off the rug, and a very dark tone in the center will create a visual hole.

Rugs with light colors at the outer band will appear larger than rugs with a very dark color at the outside edge.

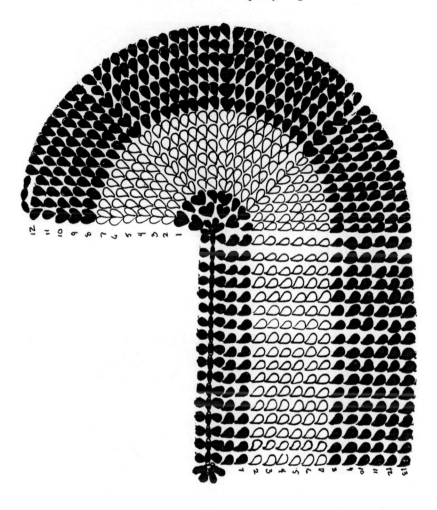

If you are using three tones of the same color (for example, light, medium and dark blue) you can arrange the bands with the light tone in the center band, the medium tone in the middle band, and the dark tone in the outer band. Variations of the wide band pattern include: using narrow bands of color between the wide bands; using all different widths of bands of color from narrow to wide in order of width or in random order; and softening the transition between bands of colors by mixing the two colors of adjacent bands for two or three rounds between the bands. This last one is called 'blended bands' and you need to prepare special balls of strip alternating strips from the two colors to work the transition.

The hit-or-miss pattern is one of the most popular of the crocheted rag rug patterns in the past. Traditionally, all the strips are cut, and placed in a large box and mix them up. When joining the strips, each color was grabbed at random from the box. This works best when your strips are all short, particularly using recycled clothing as in the rug above. Or you can prepare two similar fabrics at the same time, joining a strip of each one alternately and have bi-color balls of strip which are fun to work with. The rug below was made that way.

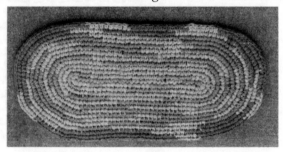

For better control of the design and colors, the fabrics should be prepared individually and kept as separate balls. Then you can change color each row creating a continual gradation of colors as shown in the rug below.

Sprials can also be used with the oval shape. They are made by using two or more fabrics alternately to crochet the rows of the rugs. You can begin the second fabric as you crochet the second side of the base chain so that the spiral extends all of the way through the rug. (See photo below.)

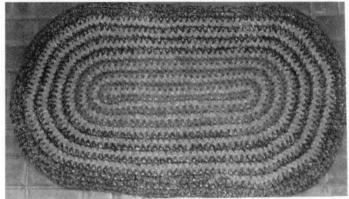

Another option is to use a spiral as a band of a wide band rug, where the second fabric is only used for a part of the rug. Try to begin and end the second fabric at about the same point around the rug to keep it from being lopsided. This type of spiral is shown in the charted pattern on the following page.

Charted Pattern for an Oval Rug with a Spiral Band

Begin the second fabric with two chain stitches, and end with two slip stitches. The first fabric is worked alternately with the second fabric while keeping the increase pattern consistent.

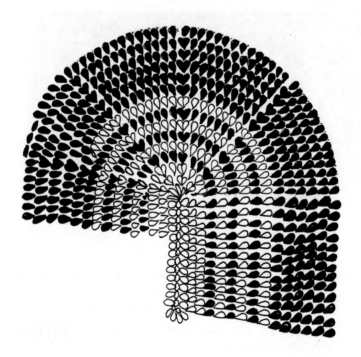

Just like the round crocheted rugs, ovals can also be made with double-spirals (using three fabrics alternately) or even more fabrics. The more fabrics used in a spiral, the more careful you need to be about making sure the paired stitches are where they need to be. It is a good idea to keep each pair marked with a safety pin as you work.

In double-spirals, end two of the fabrics at opposite ends of the rug on the same row. Then crochet the final row with only one fabric to keep a solid edge.

CHAPTER 6

OVAL FABRIC TAPESTRY RUGS

Just like round rugs, the simplest fabric tapestry patterns for oval rugs are those that are based on the paired stitches. The same sorts of "pinwheel" patterns that are used in round rugs can also be made in the oval shape.

However, the pattern lines formed along the sides of an oval will be fairly straight while around the ends, they will curve counter-clockwise, just like round rugs. For short ovals, like the "Graded Pinwheel" (on the next page) the difference hardly shows, but as the oval gets longer, the difference becomes more and more apparent.

The oval rug above is a "picket fence" design working stripes along the sides of the rug as well as in the paired stitches at the ends. Straight lines such as these can make a design awkward. For oval rugs, it is sometimes wisest to use a different, but related, design in the ends of the rugs than for the sides. (The 23" X 38" oval above used 6 yards of dark fabric and 10 yards of light fabric.)

Oval Graded Pinwheel

Compare the round graded pinwheel rug in Chapter 4 with this oval variation. These oval rugs work best with a short base chain. This 24" X 35" oval used 9 yards dark fabric, 3.5 yards medium fabric, and 3 yards light fabric)

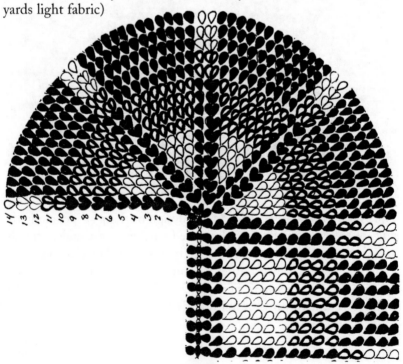

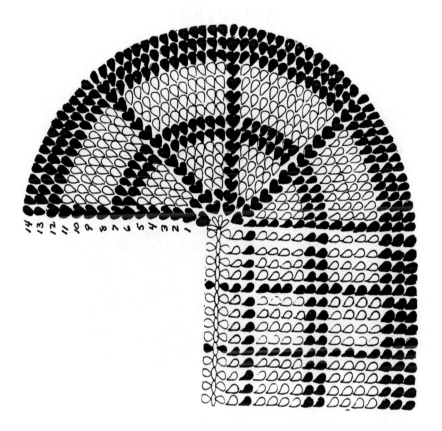

Charted Pattern for 24" X 42" oval in Tiffany Pattern

Just as in the round shape, this design is most effective if you use different solid colors for the sections between the dark lines.

CHAPTER 7

SQUARE RUGS

34-inch square fabric tapestry rug, using 28 yards of fabric, 14 each of two colors

To make a square or rectangular rug, you will need to learn a different pattern of increases than for the round and oval shapes. The square shape is formed by placing two pairs of stitches at each corner. Notice that there are still eight pairs of stitches in each row, but on squares these pairs are grouped at the corners.

At the corners of a square rug, the pairs of stitches are always inserted in the same manner. The first pair of stitches is <u>always</u> inserted into the center of the first pair of the previous round. The second pair of stitches is inserted into the very next space.

With only a little practice, you will have this pattern quickly memorized. Once you understand the placement of the increases at the corners, there is no need to count the stitches between pairs in each row.

If you will recall, on round rugs, the row called Row '1' had one single crochet stitch between each pair of stitches. The Row '2' had two stitches, etc. On a square rug there are always an even number of single crochet stitches between the corner pairs. Therefore Row '2' will have two single crochet stitches between the corner pairs. The very next row will be Row '4', then Row '6' and so on. There will never be an odd numbered row.

Estimating yardage for square rugs.
It takes a bit more fabric to make a square rug than a round rug of the same size. For common sizes, the chart below can be used as a guide.

Size	Yards of 44- or 45-inch cotton fabric
15-inch chair pad	5 yards
24-inch rug	11-12
30-inch rug	18-20
36-inch rug	26-28
42-inch rug	37-39

Basic directions for a 34-inch square rug
Prepare 24 yards of 44- to 45-inch cotton fabric for crocheting. (See "The Basics" or the Handbook section.)

Center:
(If you know how to start a round rug (or hotpad) you also know how to 'start' a square. At the very center they are identical, so you can follow the step-by-step directions for round rugs, but don't make Row '1', instead, skip to Row '2' below.)

Make a slip knot, Chain four and slip stitch into the first chain to form a ring. Chain 2, and make 7 single crochet stitches into the center of the ring.

Working in a spiral (do not chain up between rows) insert two single crochet stitches into the last chain stitch, and two single crochet stitches in each space around the row. (eight total pairs of stitches, for 16 stitches in all.)

Chart showing the center of a square rug completed with eight pairs of stitches.

Row '2': *2SC in each next 2 spaces, 1SC in each of next 2 spaces* and repeat the directions between the *'s around four times (4X) for a total of 24 stitches.

In Row '2', notice that the first pair of stitches that you make will line up with a pair from the previous row. The next pair doesn't!

The arrows in the chart point to the lined-up pairs.

Then there must be two individual single crochet stitches before you make the next pair of stitches. Look carefully at the charts and follow the written directions for Row '2' so you make sure this row is completed the right way.

As you continue, remember that the first pair at each corner <u>always</u> lines up with the first pair in the previous row.

Row '4': *2SC in each next 2 spaces, 1SC in each of next 4 spaces* repeat * around (4X)

Row '6': *2SC in each next 2 spaces, 1SC in each of next 6 spaces* repeat * around (4X)

Row '8': *2SC in each next 2 spaces, 1SC in each of next 8 spaces* repeat * around (4X)

Row '10': *2SC in each next 2 spaces, 1SC in each of next 10 spaces* repeat * around (4X)

Row '12': *2SC in each next 2 spaces, 1SC in each of next 12 spaces* repeat * around (4X)

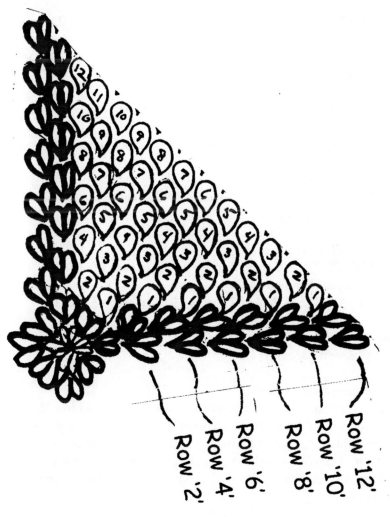

Row '14': *2SC in each next 2 spaces, 1SC in each of next 14 spaces* repeat * around (4X)
Row '16': *2SC in each next 2 spaces, 1SC in each of next 16 spaces* repeat * around (4X)

Row '18': *2SC in each next 2 spaces, 1SC in each of next 18 spaces* repeat * around (4X)
Row '20': *2SC in each next 2 spaces, 1SC in each of next 20 spaces* repeat * around (4X)

Row '22': *2SC in each next 2 spaces, 1SC in each of next 22 spaces* repeat * around (4X)
Row '24': *2SC in each next 2 spaces, 1SC in each of next 24 spaces* repeat * around (4X)

Row '26': *2SC in each next 2 spaces, 1SC in each of next 26 spaces* repeat * around (4X)
Row '28': *2SC in each next 2 spaces, 1SC in each of next 28 spaces* repeat * around (4X)

Row '30': *2SC in each next 2 spaces, 1SC in each of next 30 spaces* repeat * around (4X)
Row '32': *2SC in each next 2 spaces, 1SC in each of next 32 spaces* repeat * around (4X)
Row '34': *2SC in each next 2 spaces, 1SC in each of next 34 spaces* repeat * around (4X)
Row '36': *2SC in each next 2 spaces, 1SC in each of next 36 spaces* repeat * around (4X)
Row '38': *2SC in each next 2 spaces, 1SC in each of next 38 spaces* repeat * around (4X)

Continuing a square rug.
You probably quit reading the written directions around row '8' because you could see that each corner was easy to spot so you knew where to place the pairs of stitches. If however, you want to continue with counting the stitches in each row, the next row would be Row '40', followed by Row '42', and so on, always with even numbers.

Ending a square rug.
If you will remember, on round and oval rugs the very last round of stitching was done without using any pairs of stitches. This is **not** the case with square rugs. The two pairs at each corner are always used, even in the very last row.

You can end off a square rug at any corner without distorting its shape. For the last three spaces before you get to the corner, insert slip stitches instead of single crochet. Pull up the end of the fabric strip through the last stitch, and then lace it back into the work. Sew it down.

Square Fabric Tapestry Patterns

Like the round shape, the easiest fabric tapestry patterns are based around the paired stitches. The "Banded Cross" is similar to the pinwheell patterns in that the paired stitches are made in contrasting colors from the balance of the rug. A Banded Cross Rug is shown below and the chart for chairpads follows. There are any number of variations to the Banded Cross, including eliminating the "bands" so that the rug design is simply a large "X" shape.

21-inch square rug using 7 yards dark fabric and 5 yards light fabric

15" Banded Cross' Chairpads .
Prepare 2-1/2 yards each of a dark and light cotton fabric (5 yards total for each chairpad).

Look at the charted pattern. Begin the square as usual using just the dark fabric. Starting at Row '2' use the dark fabric just for the pairs of stitches, and the light fabric for the individual stitches. Continue this way through Row '8'.

For Rows '10 and '12', use just the dark fabric. At Row '14' again make the pairs with the dark fabric and use the light fabric for the individual stitches.

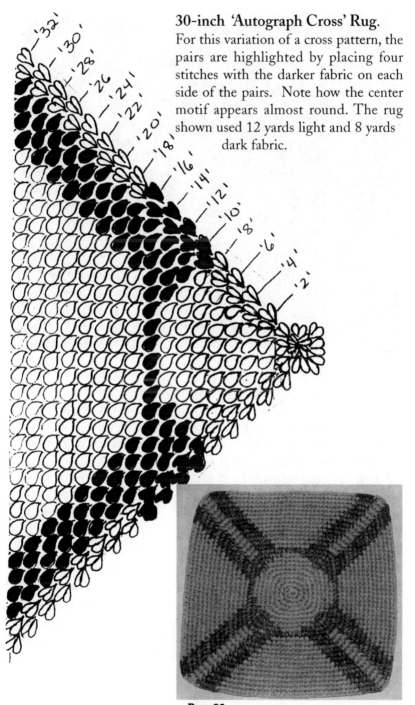

30-inch 'Autograph Cross' Rug.

For this variation of a cross pattern, the pairs are highlighted by placing four stitches with the darker fabric on each side of the pairs. Note how the center motif appears almost round. The rug shown used 12 yards light and 8 yards dark fabric.

Log Cabin Rugs

Another simple fabric tapestry pattern for the square (and rectangular) shapes is the "Log Cabin" named after the similar quilt pattern. To create the design, the colors are changed at alternating corners, with the first pair of one color and the second pair of the next color. Each color is carried for two rows. More elaborate log cabin designs can be made by changing colors at each corner in the same way.

"Nine Patch" Rug Patterns

For a country look, it is hard to beat the Nine Patch patterns whether square or rectangular. (See photo and chart.) Don't be put off that it looks complicated, because it really isn't. First notice that all of the paired stitches at the corners are done with the dark fabric. Then all you have to do is remember that all of the squares are done in "fours": four stitches wide and four rows high. If you can remember to count the "fours" you'll always know when to switch colors.

You don't have to have lots of two particular colors to make a nine patch. This is a rug that I used up a whole lot of tag ends of fabric in. The strips got sorted into generally light and generally dark fabric for the squares, and the rug ended up *very* colorful. You can also plan Nine Patch rugs with different colors used for each set of squares, or combine the Nine Patch with other quilt motifs. This is the center of a Patchwork Sampler Rug where the squares were made in different colors.

The basic Nine Patch rug is made with only two colors alternating to form a checkerboard. Above is a basic rug and opposite is the charted pattern. This 28" X 28" rug used 9 yards dark and 6 yards light fabric.

Below is a rug using the Nine Patch pattern for the center and the outer border.

Nine Patch Rugs

These rugs are easy if you remember the
"fours" since each square is four stitches
wide and four rows tall.

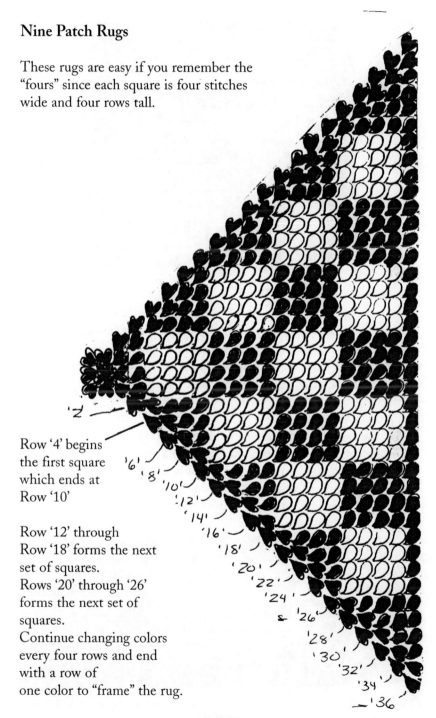

Row '4' begins
the first square
which ends at
Row '10'

Row '12' through
Row '18' forms the next
set of squares.
Rows '20' through '26'
forms the next set of
squares.
Continue changing colors
every four rows and end
with a row of
one color to "frame" the rug.

Variations of the Nine Patch

Above is a variation using large squares that are six stitches wide and six rows tall. Each large square has a smaller square inside that is two stitches wide and two rows tall. I didn't like this rug when I made it since it didn't have the formal geometry of the 4X4 squares, but it would fit right in with primitive quilts such as the ones from Gee's Bend.

Since the next chapter discusses making rectangular rugs, below is a Nine Patch variation in that shape. Nine Patch patterns work very well too in rectangular rugs, but make sure that your base chain is in a multiple of four! On this rug I extended the length of the squares to 8 rows, and added a bit of decoration to the edges.

CHAPTER 8

RECTANGULAR RUGS

Just as an oval rug is two half circles separated by straight sections of stitching, a rectangular rug is two halves of a square separated by straight sections of stitching.

A rectangular rug is begun with a chain of stitches which are <u>not</u> joined to make a circle. The length of the base chain will determine the dimensions of the rug (the difference between its width and length). If you want a rug which is three feet wide and five feet long you will want to begin with a base chain that is two feet long. (5' - 3' = 2')

We'll start with a small (18" X 24") rectangle. This is about the size of a piano bench. Remember that you can make a rectangle of any size by varying the length of the base chain. The rectangle is just as easy to follow as the square, once you have placed your corner stitches properly.

A rectangular rug is begun exactly the same way as an oval rug, so you can follow those step-by-step directions through the base row, but don't make Row '1'. Instead skip to Row '2' in the following directions.

Basic Charted Pattern for Rectangular Rugs

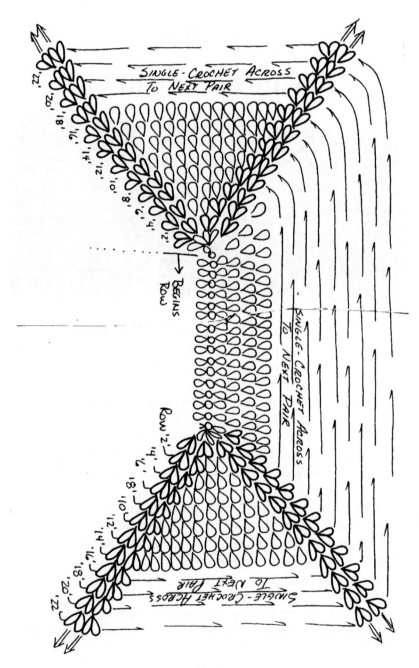

SINGLE-CROCHET ACROSS
TO NEXT PAIR

BEGINS
ROW

SINGLE-CROCHET ACROSS
TO NEXT PAIR

ROW '2', '4', '6', '8', '10', '12', '14', '16', '18', '20', '22'

SINGLE-CROCHET ACROSS
TO NEXT PAIR

Basic Rectangular Rug Directions
18" X 24" rug or bench pad.

Prepare 9 yards of 44- or 45-inch wide cotton fabric for crocheting.

Make a slip knot and Chain 17. Insert the hook into the second chain from the hook and insert one single crochet stitch into each chain (SC15). This will leave the original slip knot.

Into the slip knot insert four single crochet stitches. These stitches will bring you around the end so that you can work on the opposite side of the chain.

Insert a single crochet stitch to match up with each of the 15 single crochets on the first side. This will bring you to the two chain stitches at the end. Insert four total single crochet stitches in these chain stitches.

Row '2': *SC 16, 2SC in each of the next 2 spaces, SC in the next 2 spaces, 2SC in each of the next 2 spaces, SC in next space* Repeat * to complete second side.

Note that the first pair of stitches will line up with the four single crochets at the end. There will be two pairs of stitches at each corner, and just like the square, you will always line up the first pair of stitches with the first pair in the previous round.

Here are the written out directions for the rows necessary for the 18" X 24" rug, but if you have learned the square pattern, and have set your corners, you won't need them.

Row '4': *SC 17, 2SC in each next 2 spaces, SC in next 4 spaces, 2SC in each next 2 spaces, SC in next 2 spaces* repeat *

Row '6': *SC 18, 2SC in each next 2 spaces, SC in next 6 spaces, 2SC in each next 2 spaces, SC in next 3 spaces* repeat *

Row '8': *SC 19, 2SC in each next 2 spaces, SC in next 8 spaces, 2SC in each next 2 spaces, SC in next 4 spaces* repeat *

Page 92Row '10': *SC 20, 2SC in each next 2 spaces, SC in next 10 spaces, 2SC in each next 2 spaces, SC in next 5 spaces* repeat *

Row '12': *SC 21, 2SC in each next 2 spaces, SC in next 12 spaces, 2SC in each next 2 spaces, SC in next 6 spaces* repeat *

Row '14': *SC 22, 2SC in each next 2 spaces, SC in next 14 spaces, 2SC in each next 2 spaces, SC in next 7 spaces* repeat *

Row '16': *SC 23, 2SC in each next 2 spaces, SC in next 16 spaces, 2SC in each next 2 spaces, SC in next 8 spaces* repeat *

Row '18': *SC 24, 2SC in each next 2 spaces, SC in next 18 spaces, 2SC in each next 2 spaces, SC in next 9 spaces* repeat *

Row '20': *SC 25, 2SC in each next 2 spaces, SC in next 20 spaces, 2SC in each next 2 spaces, SC in next 10 spaces* repeat *

Row '22': *SC 26, 2SC in each next 2 spaces, SC in next 22 spaces, 2SC in each next 2 spaces, SC in next 11 spaces* repeat *

For larger rectangles, simply continue the same pattern, with Row '24' next, followed by Row '26', '28', '30' and so on.

On the last round of a rectangular rug, you will want to always end at a corner, just like a square rug.

Rectangular Fabric Tapestry Patterns
The basic fabric tapestry patterns for square rugs are all adaptable to rectangular rugs. The photo at the beginning of the chapter is of a rectangle in the Log Cabin pattern. The Banded Cross also works easily as a rectangle.

More advanced fabric tapestry patterns are also ideal for the rectangular shape--particularly letters and borders--since the rows of stitching are straight across the ends and the sides.

CHAPTER 9
COMBINED SHAPES:
CORNER AND HEART RUGS

Once you have mastered the "basic" shapes (round, oval, square and rectangle), it is easier to create other shapes by altering or combining the basic shapes. As a simple example, you can begin an oval rug and make one end round and the other with square corners. (Using a basic Tiffany pattern and brilliant colors in this shape makes a design I called the "Cathedral Window".)

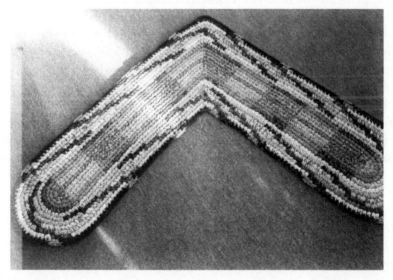

To make more complex shapes, there are some basic processes that you need to understand. The first of these is how to make a right-angle bend in a rug. "Corner Rugs" are both unique and practical so they are first. Corner rugs are begun with a base chain as if for a long oval or rectangle. The chain should be an odd number of stitches. Find and mark the center chain stitch with a safety pin. (For example if you have a base chain of 81 stitches, mark chain number 41. It will have 40 chains on each side of it.

This rug is 17 inches wide and each leg is 38 inches long. Used a total of 25 yards of fabric.

Then chain 2 and single crochet back along the chain. Place a pair of single crochet stitches in the marked center chain. Continue crocheting along the base chain. Turn the corner and crochet back as you would to begin an oval. When you reach the marked chain, *skip it*. When working with fabric strip, do not use the usual "decrease" procedure, just skip the stitch. Then continue along to the end.

Outside Corners

You will notice that the base now has a distinct bend in the center. From this point forward, the right angle is formed by inserting **two pairs of stitches at the outer bend**. These are done just like any square corner with the first pair lined up with the first pair in the previous row and the second pair inserted in the following space.

Inside Corners

For the inside corner on every round, **skip two stitches**—the ones on either side of the corner.

Other than the procedure for the corner itself, corner rugs are made just like any regular oval or rectangular rug. If you look at the photos, you'll notice that both rugs are relatively long compared to their width. To keep the "corner" impression, you need to plan that sort of ratio.

When an oval corner rug is made with a shorter base chain—you create a heart shaped rug.

Heart Shaped Rugs

It is easiest to think of a heart shaped rug as an oval rug with a bend in the middle of it. Actually this is how a heart shaped rug is made. It is begun just as if it were and oval rug, with a straight base chain and the bend is made by adding increases on one side of the base chain and decreases on the other side. The rounded lobes of the heart are made by following the same pattern of increases as an oval rug.

To simplify discussion of the heart shape the following terms are used and relate to the parts of the shape shown:

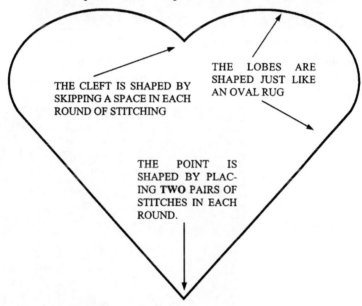

THE CLEFT IS SHAPED BY SKIPPING A SPACE IN EACH ROUND OF STITCHING

THE LOBES ARE SHAPED JUST LIKE AN OVAL RUG

THE POINT IS SHAPED BY PLACING **TWO** PAIRS OF STITCHES IN EACH ROUND.

Just as in an oval rug, the length of the initial chain of stitches affects the finished size of the rug. However, because of the special requirements of the heart shape, the base chain must also take into consideration the finished size of the planned rug. For instance a small heart shaped rug that is begun with too long of a base chain will end up looking like a corner rug instead of a true heart shape. A large rug that is begun with too short of a chain will have the cleft close up and the rug will end up in a tear drop shape instead of a heart shape.

On this page is proof that I had to learn the hard way about shaping and designing heart rugs. The rug above is of flannel and the base chain was too long which left the heart still looking like a corner rug. (Actually, I ran out of fabric so I couldn't correct the proportions.)

This heart just didn't have a long enough base chain. Note how the cleft has all but disappeared.

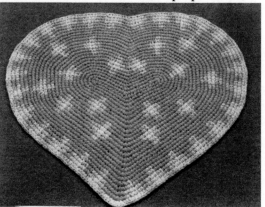

This rug had two major problems. The base chain wasn't long enough and the heart motifs in fabric tapestry were just too large for the size of the rug. With problems like these, it is best just to pull the stitches out and start over.

As a general rule heart shaped rugs which are planned to be less than 24 inches overall should be begun with a chain of 11 stitches; rugs of 24 to 30 inches across should be begun with a base chain of 21 stitches; rugs 36 to 48 inches overall should be begun with a base chain of 31 stitches.

Heart shaped rugs will have approximately the same dimensions when measured from the sides of the lobes and from the top of the lobes to the tip of the point. A heart shaped rug will require about 10% less fabric than a square rug of the same size. So to estimate the amount of fabric for a heart rug, you can use the chart for square rugs. Remember that the chart is for estimated yardages using 1-1/2 inch strips of cotton fabrics. The actual yardages will vary depending on the fabric you choose, the surface design you choose and your individual crochet touch.

In the heart shape, the lobes are made just as if they were the ends of an oval rug, with four pairs of stitches on each lobe. The row numbers indicate how many individual crochet stitches separate the pairs of stitches at each row. For instance, in Row '1' there will be one individual crochet stitch separating each pair of stitches located at the lobes. In Row '2', there will be two individual stitches and so on.

The point of the heart is made by adding increases (pairs of stitches) in each round. The point is begun with a pair of stitches in the middle of the base chain on one side, and skipping the matching space on the other side of the base chain. In all subsequent rounds, the point is made just exactly like a corner on a square rug. There are two pairs of stitches inserted at the point. The first pair of stitches will line up with the first pair in the previous round.

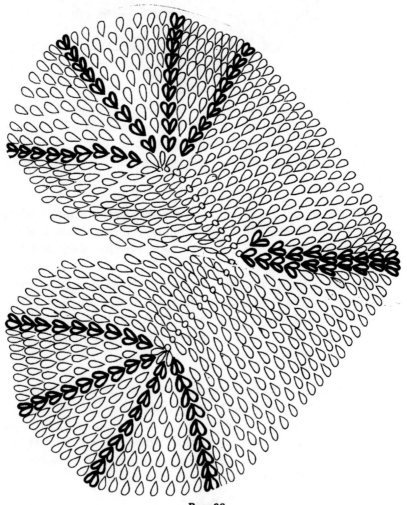

The cleft of the heart is made by skipping stitches for decreases. This is different than a standard decrease in crochet where two spaces are worked into the same stitch. Because of the bulk of fabric strip, a space is simply skipped. Otherwise a bulky bulge is created.

The lobes of the heart are made exactly like the ends of an oval rug (in other words, each end is a half circle). The most critical point in crocheting a heart shaped rug is at the very beginning. You must identify the middle stitch in the base of chain stitches accurately to know where to begin decreasing for the cleft and increasing for the point. If you begin these features at the wrong chain stitch, the heart will be lop-sided.

Because the standard written directions for heart rugs are so messy, once you get through Row '1', you will find it easier to work with the charted pattern.

Directions: 27 inch heart shaped rug

Requires 10 yards of 45" cotton fabric, cut into 1-1/2 inch strips as in the chapter on fabric preparation. Use a Size K or L crochet hook. To Crochet:

27 inch heart-shaped rug:
Begin at center, make a slip knot.
Chain 21 (this is the base chain), then chain 2 more (this is to turn the corner) Mark the 11ᵗʰ chain from the start with a safety pin.
Core: Working back along the chain, insert the hook into the second chain from the hook, SC in next 10 chains, then SKIP next chain (this is the middle stitch and begins the cleft of the heart). SC in next 10 chains, 4 SC into original slip know, SC in next 10 chains, 2 SC in next chain (this is teh middle stitch and this pair of stitches begins the point of the heart). SC in next 10 chains, 4 SC into last chain.

Base: SC in next 9 SC, skip next SC, SC in next SC, skip next SC, SC in next 9 SC, 2 SC in each next 4 SC, SC in next 10 SC, 2 SC in each next 2 SC, SC in next 9 SC, 2 SC in each next 4 SC.

Row '1': SC in next 8 SC, skip next space, SC in next SC, skip next SC, SC in next 9 SC, 2 SC in next SC, SC in next SC, 2 SC in next SC, SC in next SC, 2 SC in next SC, SC in next SC, 2 SC in next SC, SC in next 11, SC, 2 SC in each next 2 SC, SC in next 11 SC, 2 SC in next SC, SC in next SC, 2 SC in next SC, SC in next SC, 2 SC in next SC, SC in next SC, 2 SC in next SC.

Row '2': SC in next 8 SC, skip next SC, SC in next SC, skip next SC SC in next 8 SC 2 SC in next SC, SC in next 2 SC, 2 SC in next SC, SC in next 2 SC, 2 SC in next SC, SC in next 2 SC, 2 SC in next SC, SC in next 12 SC, 2 SC in each next 2 SC, SC in next 13 SC, 2 SC in next SC, SC in next 2 SC, 2 SC in next SC, SC in next 2 SC, 2 SC in next SC, SC in next 2 SC, 2 SC in next SC.

Row '3': SC in next 7 SC, skip next SC, SC in nextSC, skip next SC, SC in next 8 SC, *2 SC in next SC, SC in next 3 SC, 2 SC in next SC, SC in next 3 SC, 2 SC in next SC, SC in next 3 SC, 2 SC in next SC* SC in next 14 SC, 2 SC in each next 2 SC, SC in next 14 SC, repeat section between *'s

Row '4': SC in next 7 SC, skip next space, SC in next SC, skip next space, SC in next 7 SC, * 2 SC in next SC, SC in next 4 SC, 2 SC in next SC, SC in next 4 SC, 2 SC in next SC, SC in next4 SC, 2 SC in next SC*, SC in next 15 SC, 2 SC in each next 2 SC, SC in next 16 SC, repeat section between *'s.

Row '5': SC in next 7 SC, skip next space, SC in next SC, skip next space, SC in next 6 SC, *2 SC in next SC, SC innext 5 SC, 2 SC in next SC, SC in next 5 SC, 2 SC in next SC, SC in next 5 SC, 2 SC i next SC*, SC in next 17 SC, 2 SC in each next 2 SC, SC in next 17 SC, repeat section between *'s.

Row '6': SC in next 6 SC, skip next space, SC in next SC, skip next SC, SC in next 6 SC, * 2 SC in next SC, SC in next 6 SC, 2 SC in next SC, SC in next 6 SC, 2 SC in next SC, SC in next 6 SC, 2 SC in next SC*, SC in next 18 SC, 2 SCin each next 2 SC, SC in next 19 SC, repeat section between *'s.

Row '7': SC in next 6 SC, skip next space, C in next SC, skip next SC, SC in next 5 SC, *2 SC in next SC, SC in next 7 SC, 2 SC in next SC, SC in next 7 SC, 2 SC in next SC, SC in next 7 SC, 2 SC in next SC*, Sc in next 20 SC, 2 SC in each next 2 SC, SC in next 20 SC, repeat section between *'s.

Row '8': SC in next 5 SC, skip next space, SC in next SC, skip next SC, SC in next 5 SC, *2 SC in next SC, SC in next 8 SC, 2 SC in next SC, SC in next 8 SC, 2 SC in next SC, SC in next 8 SC, 2 SC in next SC*, SC in next 21 SC, 2 SC in each next 2 SC, SC in next 22 SC, repeat section between *'s.

Row '9': SC in next 5 SC, skip next space, SC in next SC, skip next SC, SC in next 4 SC, *2 SC in next SC, SC in next 9 SC, 2 SC in next SC, SC in next 9 SC, 2 SC in next SC, SC in next 9 SC, 2 SC in next SC*, SC in next 23 SC, 2 SC in each next 2 SC, SC in next 23 SC, repeat section between *'s

Your heart should have taken shape sufficiently that you can let the rug be your guide in continuing to work through rows '10' ,11' and '12' with those numbers of individual single crochet stitches between the pairs in the lobes of the heart. Always skip two spaces at the cleft of the heart and make two pairs of stitches at the point of the heart.

For the final row at the outside edge, do not use any pairs of stitches around the lobes of the heart, but DO continue to skip the spaces at the cleft of the heart and put two pairs of stitches at the point of the heart. Try to end the last row around the curve of a lobe or at the very point with three slip stitches. Pull the strip up through the last loop and (with a lacing needle) work it back into the rug. Sew the end in place and clip off any excess.

The neatest edge finish is made using a lacing needle an making a whip stitch with fabric strip all the way around the rug. Especially at the point of the heart, the stitches will be best proteched with a whip stitch edge.

FOR LARGER HEARTS

The general directions and the charted pattern will make a heart rug about 27 or 28 inches across. To make larger rugs, you will need to use a longer base chain, or the cleft of the heart will fill in and the rug will lose its heart appearance.

For each additional inch in width that you plan, add two more chain stitches to the base chain. Also, with larger heart rugs, to maintain a rounded edge at the lobes, the paired stitches should be shifted around similarly to making a round crocheted rug (instead of an octagon).

Starting Small with a Heart Shaped Potholder

The heart shape can be intimidating the first time that you try it, so for years I've suggested this project as a way to gain confidence with hearts. This pattern first appeared in our catalog in 1985. The potholder is 9" X 7" overall with its own hanger. You will need 7/8 yard of 45" wide cotton fabric, cut into strips 3/4" wide and sewn to make a continuous length. This is quick project that will let you practice the heart shape (and also a dandy gift or bazaar item).

Use size J or K crochet hook.

Make a slip knot and chain 13.

Begin at second chain from hook. SC5, skip next chain, SC5, 4SC into slip knot, SC5, 2SC in next space, SC5, 4SC in last Chain.

Base: SC4, skip 1, SC5, 2SC in each of next 4 spaces, SC5, 2SCin each of next 2 spaces, SC5, 2SC in each of next 4 spaces, SC5

Round 1: SC4, Skip 1, SC5. *For the next seven spaces insert the following in order: 2SC, 1SC, 2SC, 1SC, 2SC, 1SC, 2SC.* SC6, 2SC in each of next 2 spaces, SC 7. Repeat the sequence of seven*

Round 2: SC4, skip 1, SC 5. *For next 10 stitches alternate 2SC, then 1SC, 1SC*. SC7, 2SC in each of next 2 spaces, SC9. Repeat the sequence of 10*

Round 3: SC4, Skip 1, SC5. *For next 13 stitches alternate 2SC, then 1SC, 1SC, 1SC.* SC8, 2SC in each of next 2 spaces, SC11. Repeat the sequence of 13*

Round 4: SC4, skip 1, SC29, 2SC, SC32, Slip 1, skip 1, slip 10.

Hanger: Chain 10, Slip 2, end off and lace end of strip back into work. Sew strip end in place.

Variations of the Crocheted Heart Potholder

Hotpad: This pattern will work with "standard fabric strip" (1-1/2 inches wide). With the wider strip the potholder will become a heavier "hotpad"—like a miniature rug—and will be slightly larger also. Use a size L or N hook, and allow 1-1/4 yards of 45" fabric (about 35 yards of strip). Then just follow the pattern above.

Basket: With the 1-1/2 inch fabric strip, this pattern can also be used to create a heart shaped rag basket. Follow the above pattern though round 4. Then just single crochet around and around the heart (one stitch in each space) to make the sides of the basket. Allow about 1-3/4 yards of 45" fabric (about 50 yards of strip). There is a photo of a heart-shaped basket in the Handbook section.

CHAPTER 10

COMBINED SHAPES HEELPRINT, PENTAGON, ROUND/SQUARE

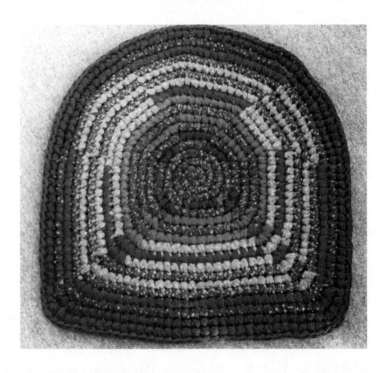

In the previous chapter, basic shapes were combined with a right-angle to make new forms. In this chapter, two different shapes are combined to create a completely new shape. Round and square shapes used together, create a heelprint shape. An octagon worked with alternately too few and too many increases creates a pentagonal rug, and finally combining round and square shapes alternately creates a rug with unique design potential. All of the directions in this chapter are for basic rugs in specialty shapes. Any of these rugs can be made more elaborate by using fabric tapestry techniques.

HEELPRINT RUGS

Heelprint rugs are made by combining two basic rug shapes: the round and the square. The paired stitches on the round half of the rug follow the basic round pattern. On the other half of the rug, the paired stitches are set up just as for a square rug.

Heel print rugs can be made in any size, however, they are ideally suited as chairpads for captain's chairs where the seats are curved at the back and straight across the front.

On the previous page is a 24" X 24" Heel Print rug, in a dappled pattern mixing several colors. (Materials: 10-3/4 yards of 44"-45" wide fabric cut into about 300 yards of 1-1/2 inch fabric strips for crocheting.)

The paired stitches on the round part of the rug are separated by 1, then 2, then 3 individual stitches (there are four pairs of stitches in the rounded part of the rug). The paired stitches on the square portion of the rug (along the straight edge) are separated by 2, then 4, then 6, etc. individual stitches in each row. For this reason each row has two numbers: the first indicating the individual stitches on the rounded end, and the second indicating the individual stitches along the straight edge (see charted pattern).

In order to keep the rug shape symmetrical, the pairs around the curved part of the rug are moved forward a space each row. The location of the pairs does not affect the spacing between the pairs though. In row '7' for instance there are seven individual single crochet stitches between each pair around the curve.

The row numbers do not however indicate the number of stitches that form the transition between the square and round parts. This spacing is done automatically by following the progression for the pairs along the curved edge.

The basic heel print shape can be made larger by continuing the charted progression; or smaller by crocheting fewer rows. On the last row of any size heel print rug, place the double pairs at the corners as usual, but do not put any pairs around the curved portion of the rug.

Heelprint shape charted pattern

Begins Row '8' ('16')

Estimating yardages
Heel print rugs take just a bit less fabric to make than square rugs, so the same chart as for the square shape. This shape is particularly suited to chairpads for "captains chairs" which have a rounded back and a squared off front edge. (Allow five yards of fabric for each chairpad.)

Before you begin a heelprint chairpad or rug, you should have experience making both round and square crocheted projects and be comfortable with using the charted patterns for each shape. The heelprint is not the shape to choose for your first project!

HEELPRINT DIRECTIONS

(The following directions are for a 24" X 24" rug. For a chairpad follow the directions through row '11' ('22') and then make a last round without pairs on the curved edge only.)

To Crochet: Begin at center, make a slip knot, Ch4, Slip Stitch into first loop to form circle. CH 2, SC 7 into center. (Do not join rounds, work proceeds in a spiral. Mark the end of each round with a safety pin.)

Base: 2 SC into last CH and into each SC around. (16 SC in the whole round. This is just like the base for both the round and square shapes.)

Row '1' ('2'): (In this row, the square corners are worked first and they should be marked with as safety pin so that you can keep oriented to the project's shape.) 2 SC in each of the next two spaces (mark these pairs with a safety pin), SC in next 2 spaces, 2 SC in each of the next two spaces (mark these pairs with a safety pin), SC in next 2 spaces. *2 SC in next space, SC in next space* repeat between * four times in all. (This will begin the rounded section and should bring you back to the safety pin marking the first corner.)

Row '2' ('4'): In this row the corners are worked exactly like in the square shape. 2 SC in each next 2 spaces, SC in next 4 spaces, 2 SC in each next 2 spaces. Then the round edge is begun, but instead of placing the paired stitches in line with the previous row, they are inserted in the space before the pair in the previous row. SC in next 3 spaces, 2 SC in next space, SC in next 2 spaces, 2 SC in next space, SC in next 2 spaces, 2 SC in next space, SC in next 2 spaces, 2 SC in next space, SC in next 3 spaces.

Row '3' ('6'): 2 SC in each next 2 spaces, SC in next 6 spaces, 2 SC in each next 2 spaces. SC in next 4 spaces, 2 SC in next space, SC in next 3 spaces, 2 SC in next space, SC in next 3 spaces, 2 SC in next space, SC in next 3 spaces, 2 SC in next space, SC in next 5 spaces.

Row '4' ('8"): 2 SC in each next 2 spaces, SC in next 5 spaces, 2 SC in each next 2 spaces. SC in next 5 spaces, 2 SC in next space, SC in next 4
spaces, 2 SC in next space, SC in next 4 spaces, 2 SC in next space, SC in next 4 spaces, 2 SC in next space, SC in next 7 spaces.

At this point (if you haven't already) mark all of the pairs on the rounded edge with safety pins and move the pins marking the square corners up to the most recent stitches. From here on, let the pins guide you so that you don't have to follow the pattern any longer. Regularly move the pins as you work.

Along the square edge, there are always two pairs of stitches at the corner. The first pair is inserted in the first pair of the previous row, and the second pair in the space immediately following. Work one single crochet in each space along the edge. Around the rounded edge, insert a pair of stitches in the space immediately before the pair in the previous row. Make one single crochet stitch in the other spaces. If you are making a chair pad, you'll want to continue until there are about 22 stitches along the square edge between the pairs. If you are using fabric strip wider than 1-1/2 inches or heavier cotton fabric, measure the work. When it reaches about an inch smaller than the desired size, begin the last row. (For a rug about 24 inches across, the row beginning with 34 stitches will be the last row.)

For the last row, make the paired stitches as usual in the square corners, but make only single crochet stitches (no pairs) along the rounded edge. Finish with three slip stitches on the curved section, pull the end of the strip up and lace it back into the work. You can use fabric strip to whip stitch around the outside edge for a neat finish.

PENTAGONS

Pentagonal rugs start off just like a round rug through Row '1' and then five points are formed. At each point pairs of stitches are inserted: **one pair and then two pair in alternate rows.**

You can make pentagons in any size. To estimate the amount of fabric that you will need, use the chart for square rugs. Pentagons take slightly less fabric than squares.

Pentagonal rugs are ideal for fabric tapestry patterns that represent a large flower. Note in the rug above the lines of paired stitches proceed from the center to the corners. The design is worked between the pairs to define a five-petal floral shape.

Crocheting a Pentagonal Rug

Center: Make a slip knot and chain 4. Slip stitch to join to circle.

Chain 2. Into the center of the ring insert seven single crochet stitches. Working in a spiral (do not chain up) insert two single crochet stitches into each space around, for a total of 8 pairs (16 stitches).

Row '1': Insert a pair of single crochet stitches into the center of each pair of stitches in the previous round. Make one single crochet stitch in the space between each pair.

Second round: Insert a pair of single crochet stitches into the first pair of row '1', then one single crochet stitch in the next 3 spaces. *Insert a pair of single crochet stitches into the next space, then one single crochet stitch in each of the next four spaces*. Repeat the * sequence a total of four times to complete the round. Mark the paired stitches with safety pins.

Third round: At each of the five marked corners: insert a pair of single crochet stitches into the center of the pair in the previous round, and insert a pair of stitches into the very next space as well. All other spaces have one single crochet stitch.

Fourth round: At each of the five marked corners: insert a pair of single crochet stitches into the center of the first pair of stitches in the previous round. All other spaces have one single crochet stitch.

To continue: Alternate the directions for the third and fourth rounds until the rug is as large as you want.

Ending: Always end off at one of the points. Make 3 slip stitches, pull the end of the strip up through the last stitch and then lace the strip end back into the work. Sew the end in place and clip off any excess. A firmer edge an be made by using the fabric strip to whip stitch around the outside.

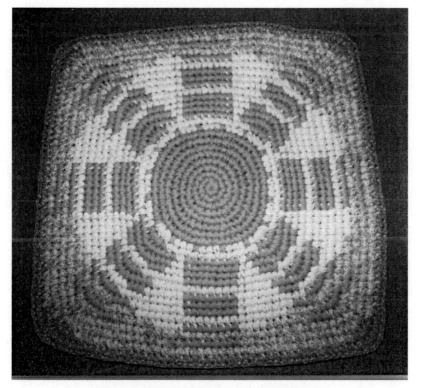

SHAPE-SHIFTING IN ONE RUG

In the rug shown above, the shape and increase pattern were changed; it was begun as a round rug, but finished as a square.

If you look at the rug closely, you can identify the changes as they were made. This was an experimental rug that I made for a solar energy themed competition (no, it didn't win) and I wanted to portray design elements that worked only in the round shape and others that worked only in the square.

I'm including this rug as a demonstration that the increase patterns for different shapes can be quite fluid. You aren't locked into following the increase pattern for just one shape at a time.

(The 28-inch rug above required 7 yards for the central motif and rays, 5 yards each for the two background colors and 2 yards for the border.)

CHAPTER 11

FREEFORM AND HOLLOW RUGS

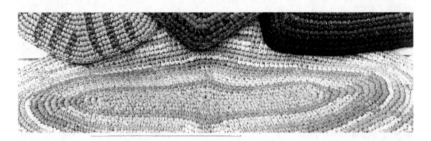

By now you've gotten the idea that by understanding the basic increase patterns, you can make a rug of almost any shape or configuration. Where the rug curves outward, there will always be four pairs of stitches to accommodate a full half turn. On inside curves, you will decrease. These rugs are only limited by your imagination.

Above is a photo of a freeform rug with a different feature. I wanted to create a rug in an ovoid shape (rounder on the sides than a standard oval). At the center of each side, a pair of stitches was added, then two pairs in the following two rows. That formed the bulge that is visible in the pattern. In the following rows, no additional pairs were needed and because the rug had the overall shape that I was after. (I apologise that I don't have good portrait of this particular rug, some just slipped past without good photographs.)

This rug is meant as an example of how you can experiment with rug shapes if you follow some basic advice.

1. For gentle outside curves, add paired stitches only as needed.

2. For sharp outer curves allow four pairs of stitches to allow for a full half-round.

3. For a right-angle outside corner, add two pairs of stitches (just like a square rug.

4. For a right-angle inside corner, skip two stitches.

5. For a less prominent outside angle, add just one pair of stitches.

6. For a less prominent inside angle, skip just one pair of stitches.

7. For symmetry on both sides of the rug, line up the inside and outside angles. (The rug above has a one-pair outside corner, and inside corner along each side.)

8. For asymmetrical rugs, outside curves and corners can be added at random, but inside corners and curves must be balanced with the opposite side of the rug, or it will not lay flat.

9. You can add a chain of stitches off the center of any rug at any point to form a projection keeping in mind that the end of the projection is treated like the end of an oval or rectangle. (You'll need four pairs of stitches at the end of the projection.) Where the projection meets the body of the rug, you will need to make an inside corner (skipping one stitch for a low angle or two stitches for a right angle).

10. You can make rugs with two or more centers by treating each center as if it were a separate rug to start with, following the increase pattern for that shape. On rounded ends, make sure that the paired stitches line up, on square corners use the two pairs. On inside corners, skip one space.

The rug above was begun as two small squares. A short chain was made off one square and then the same fabric was used to stitch around the second center. The rug was worked as a spiral (alternately crocheting with one color and then the other).

Look closely at the center of the rug. There were two low-angle inside corners at the section is begun. As the rug got larger, the two low-angle corners became a single right angle inside corner. The same situation will occur no matter what shape the original centers are.

If the rug had continued with more rounds of crocheting, eventually the inside corner would fill in (see the discussion about heart-shaped rugs). The pointed ends could also have been modified to a rounded shape in later rows resulting in an ovoid shape in the final rug.

HOLLOW RUGS

Occasionally you may want a rug that is 'hollow' in the center. For example you might want a rug that fits around the legs of a coffee table or the base of a pedestal table. In the round and square shapes these are easily made. Make a base chain that is the size of the opening that you want in the center of the rug. For a round rug, the number of chains must be divisible by 8; and for a square rug the number of chains must be divisible by four. (See the illustration on the following page.)

Join the base chain to a ring. With safety pins, mark the spaces where you will insert pairs. In the round shape, there will be eight pairs, evenly spaced around the ring. In the square shape there will be four evenly placed corners.

Chain 2, then insert a single crochet stitch into each chain stitch until you reach a marked chain. For the round shape, there will be one pair of stitches at each of the 8 marked spaces. For the square shape, there will be a pair of stitches in the two chains that form the corner.

Tricky bit! When you have finished the first round of stitching, lay the center of the rug flat, and make sure that the stitches have not twisted around the chain before you start on the next round.

Then continue, always working in a spiral just as you would for any round or square rug. For the round, there will always be eight pairs of stitches in each round of stitches. For the square rug there will always be two pairs of stitches at each corner (and the first pair will always line up with the previous round.

Oval and rectangular hollow rugs are done very much the same, except that you have to lay the base chain flat and mark the spaces for paired stitches by the look of the rug. It really helps to have another person help you hold and position the base chain so that the pairings are marked evenly.

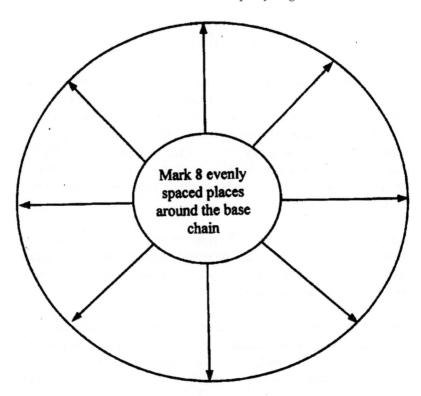

Mark 8 evenly spaced places around the base chain

Place a pair of stitches at each of the eight positions and continue as if the rug were a regular round.

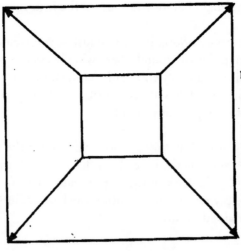

Hollow squares are made the same way. Mark FOUR evenly spaced places along the base chain, and put TWO pairs of stitches in each spot.

CHAPTER 12

NOVICE
FABRIC TAPESTRY PATTERNS

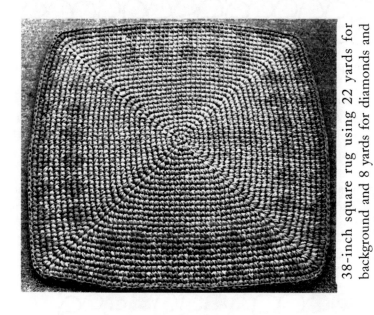

38-inch square rug using 22 yards for background and 8 yards for diamonds and sawtooth border.

In the previous chapters, beginning fabric tapestry patterns are shown along with the basic directions for crocheting a particular shape. Those patterns are all based on the paired stitches. The next step in complexity are the novice patterns which are worked in simple progressions but do require counting stitches. Because diamond and star patterns are made this way, even a novice can create striking rugs.

The most basic of the novice patterns are borders, which can be made on any shape and will add interest to any crocheted rug. Many of the simple border motifs can also be used scattered around a rug for an overall pattern.

The simplest border is of course a solid one, but the color change from background to border will show. The easiest way to diguise the change is to make a "notched" border, with two rows of fabric tapestry stitches. Alternate two stitches of the background color with two stitches of the border color for two rows, lining up the colors so that they form little squares.

Or, you can use the little squares as the border by shifting the positions of the background and border color so they form two rows of small squares as shown below.

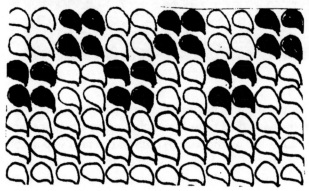

Similar to the notched border is a "sawtooth" border (top of following page) which uses small triangles begun every sixth stitch with the border color. The triangle gets wider with each row until the final row is a solid border. Triangles can be made with any spacing that you like, and they are particularly effective on round rugs (see the Poinsettia rug in the next chapter).

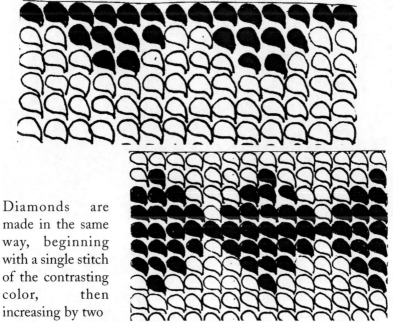

Diamonds are made in the same way, beginning with a single stitch of the contrasting color, then increasing by two in each row until the widest part of the diamond is reached, then decreasing the contrasting stitches by two until the diamond is completed. Diamonds can be used joined (as above) or as separate motifs.

Hearts are begun in the same way as diamonds, but the top of the heart is formed by two small squares. These are most effective as small motifs in the size shown in the chart. Begin the hearts six stitches apart (at a minimum). The "Home" rug later in this chapter has this type of heart border.

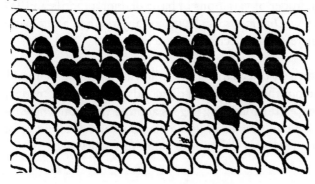

Diamond patterns can be very simple if you look at the center of the rug as a pinwheel. Shown are two diamond pattern chairpads (from the back) and a closeup of the center of one shows the pinwheel where the paired stitches are made with the light fabric and the single stitches are made with the dark fabric.

For these chairpads, the diamonds are fairly small to keep them in scale, so the pinwheel pattern is continued only until the diamonds are four stitches wide.

Then the diamonds decrease in width by one stitch in each round. If you look at the charted rug pattern on the next page, you can see the center of it is exactly the same as the chairpads.

There are any number of variations of basic diamond motifs and I've included just a few. Diamonds can be placed anywhere in a rug by the same gradual increase and decrease of stitches.

For the rug shown in the chart on the following page the diamonds are all one color, but the outer row of diamonds could also be made in a different color. On the following page is another variation where the diamonds are larger and each row in the diamonds is a different color. That progression can form the basis of some very fancy rugs.

Chart for 24-inch rug with diamonds

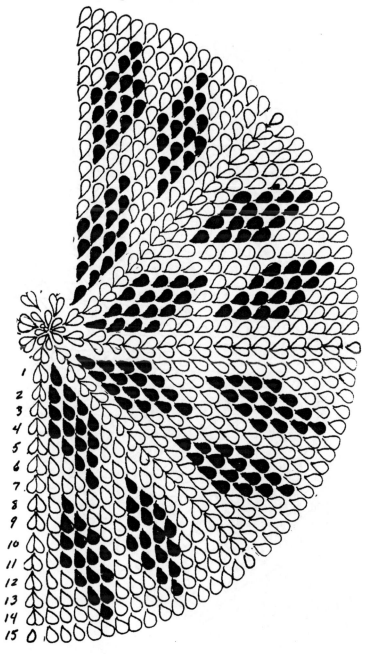

Chart for 24-inch rug with color progession in larger diamond motifs

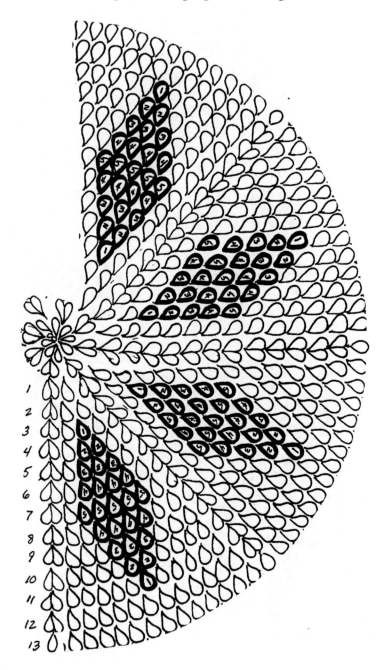

Diamond motifs can be used with any shape of rug, but they present a particular problem in oval rugs since the diamonds lay differently around the curved ends and the straight sides. Notice how they appear in the photo. You can somewhat overcome that problem by using a different approach to the diamonds along the straight sides as shown in the chart on the following page.

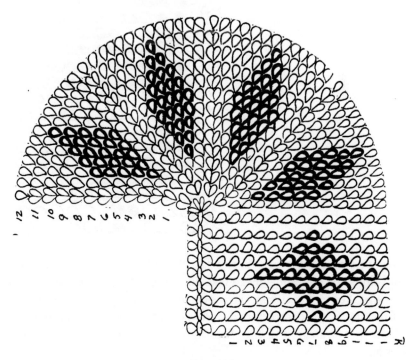

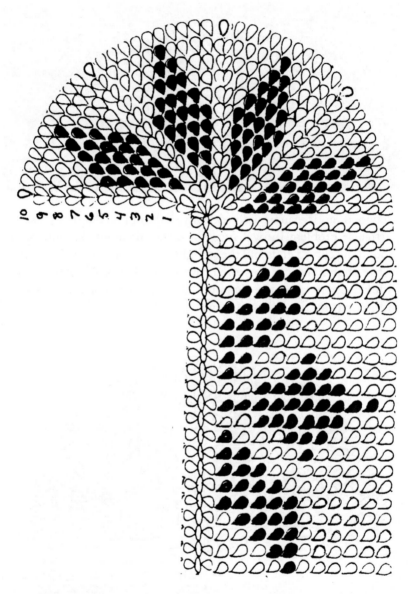

Diamond motifs for an oval rug can be made differently at the ends and along the straight sides to take advantage of the characteristics of the way the crochet stitches lay. You can also use diamonds on the end of the rug and a completely different motif along the straight sides. With that strategy, the end diamonds act as accents for the central design.

Star Patterns for Rugs

Because of the shape of stars, they are most suited to round rugs. Stars are, of course, closely related to diamonds since the "points" of the stars are made by decreasing the number of pattern stitches in each round just like the upper points of diamonds. In the rug above, the relationship is clear since the diamonds form the center of the star.

Stars are begun with a center of a solid color. At any row, the star is begun by using a contrasting color for the paired stitches (background color). By changing the background color a second time, a second star can be made as in this rug.

Charted Pattern for a Simple Star, 24-inch

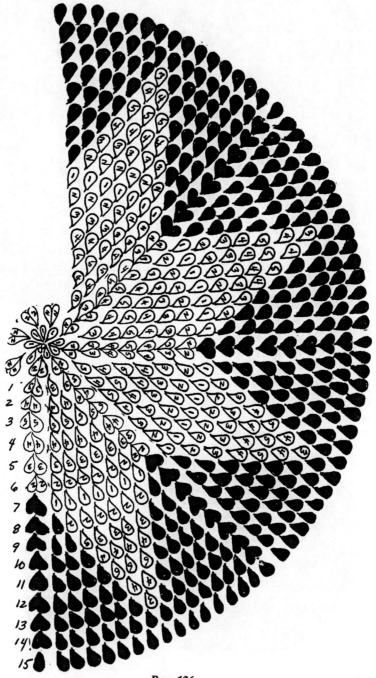

Charted Pattern for Diamonds in a Star, 24-inch

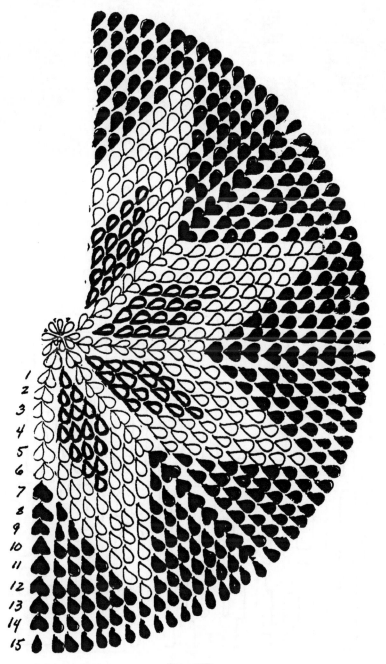

On straight sections of stitching in square rugs, or along the sides of ovals or rectangles, you can make letters. You can use most charted letters from cross-stitch patterns or design your own as long as the vertical elements are two stitches wide. The charted letters below were used in the rug above to spell out the word "HOME". All of them are ten rows tall and at least six stitches wide ("M" and "W" require eight stitches).

CHAPTER 13

INTERMEDIATE FABRIC TAPESTRY PATTERNS

Up to this point, the fabric tapestry patterns have all been made working with just two strands of fabric at a time with fairly simple motifs. In this chapter, some new tricks are introduced such as shifting pairs, working with three strands at once and more elaborate designs are introduced.

The technique of fabric tapestry with multiple strands is not more complex than working with just two strands. All of the strands that are to be hidden are held to the front of the work, and the strand for crocheting is held to the back. When you want to stitch with a different color, simply take that color to the back and bring the previous crocheting strip to the front.

You can use up to eight strands for short sections without distorting the rug, but as a general rule, only carry along the strands that are needed to work the particular row. With multiple strands you also have to be more careful not to pull on the carried strands which will also distort the rug.

Elaborate designs can be made using just three or four strands if you plan your colors carefully. Sketch the rug in color and study the number of colors needed in each row. Often just shifting the pattern one row will simplify the task of crocheting but not affect the design itself. I avoid using more than four strands if I possibly can since the balls of rug strip tangle like mad.

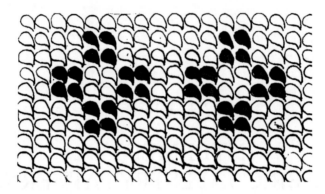

A good place to start working with three strands is the "Forget-Me-Not" motif charted above. Three strands are used: for the background; for the petals; and for the center of the motif. This pattern only requires handling three strands for the two rows that make up the center of the design.

If you look at the rugs, you'll be notice that the Forget-Me-Not is formed by five squares, each two rows high and two stitches wide.

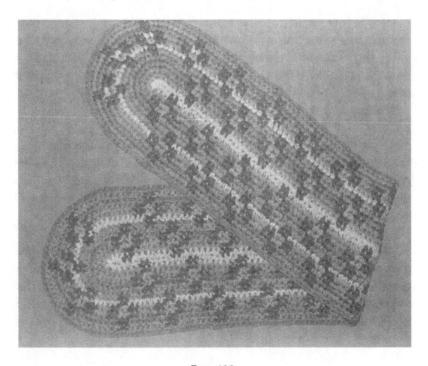

On these pages are two approaches to using the Forget-Me-Not motif. Both are long runners since the motif is very effective in long rugs. The first uses a background that is a color progression and the motifs are placed in two rows along the sides, but only one row around the end. That is because at the ends of the oval, you'll want to place the motifs only when the stitches between the pairs are wide enough to accomodate a full six stitches.

Also notice that the motifs are placed three stitches apart. They can be spaced farther apart, but placing them only two stitches apart creates an unwanted checkerboard effect.

In the rug on this page, the Forget-Me-Nots are worked on a solid back ground in a single row.

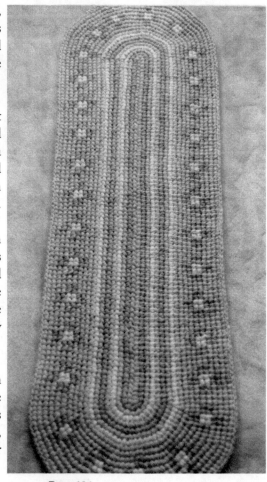

I've made quite a lot rugs with the motif and prefer a design with a blue for the petals and an ivory center on almost allbackgrounds.

They will work with any color for the petals as long as there is good contrast with the background and the center is noticeably lighter.

This rug was begun with an 80-stitch base chain and used 4 yards light, 18 yards medium, and 6 yards darker fabric.

In the chapter on freeform rugs are demonstrations of shifting paired stitches to create unique rug shapes. Pairs can also be shifted to create a particular design effect. The "Sparkling Star" is an example of this technique.

Compare the Sparkling Star to the star shaped rugs in the novice chapter. Notice that the two stars aren't lined up in the Sparkling Star, yet they retain their distinct star shapes. This is accomplished by working a regular star in the center of the rug. When that star is completed, the eight pairs of stitches are shifted around the rug (at row "8").

The second star is begun with the pairs in the new position. After the second star is completed, the pairs are shifted again (row "16"). In smaller rugs, this maintains a round shape. In a larger rug, it can be used to begin another star.

Chart for a 30-inch "Sparkling Star"
Note pairs shift positions at rows "8" and "16"

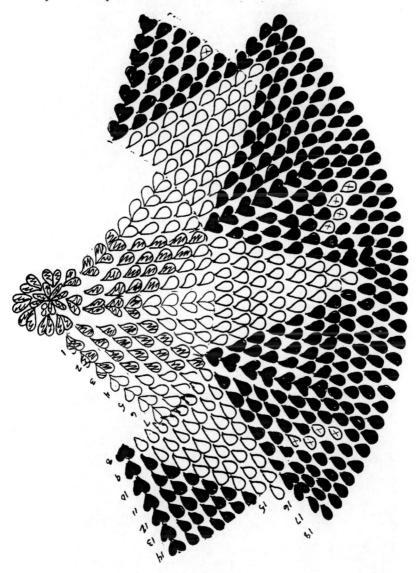

The Sparkling Star is most effective in red, white and blue. The center star being red and the outer background a deep blue. The "sparkles" are optional of course.

27-inch Pointsettia using 6.5 yards each of light and dark fabrics.

The "Pointsettia" rug has always been a favorite since it is so festive when done in colors that mimic the flower (red center motif and green for the sawtooth border with a pale pink or rose background). It is, however equally effective in many other color schemes. It is also very flexible in size. The charted pattern is for a 24-inch rug, but by adding additional rounds of the background color, larger rugs can be made in any size. Notice the extended background in the rug below.

If the inner "petals" and the outer "petals" are different colors, you will need to use three strands in the rows where they overlap.

30-inch Pointsettia using 13 yards for the background and 14 yards for the center motif and border.

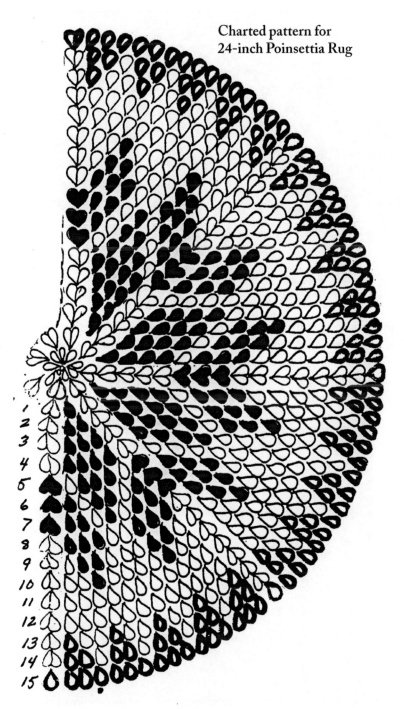

Charted pattern for
24-inch Poinsettia Rug

Above is a festive rug for the 4th of July or any folk decorating scheme. The center is a slight modification of a plain star using two strands of fabric strip. The 28-inch rug used 5 yards light, 4 yards medium and 4 yards dark fabric. The border is made with red, white and blue prints so it will require three strands through that section only.

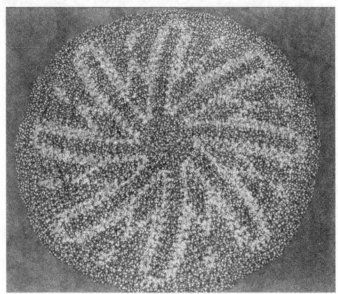

The rug at the bottom of the previous page was inspired by a motif from a bandana. It is a slightly more difficult pattern since there are two shapes that are worked at the same time: the bordered lines around the paired stitches and the hollow diamonds in the center. The charted pattern shows more clearly how the shapes are constructed.

When working with two different motifs at at the same time, it helps to cover the outer part of the pattern so that it doesn't become too confusing.

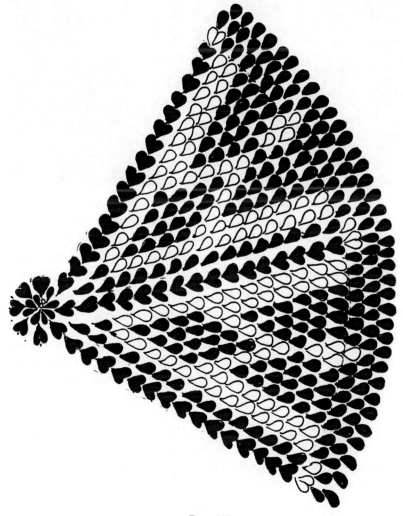

The "Star of Bethlehem"

The "Star of Bethlehem" pattern is one of the showiest of rugs. Based on the classic quilt design, it is a series of expanding stars—actually linked diamonds—just like the quilt. Despite its intricate appearance, it is not complicated to make and only requires handling two strands of fabric at a time. This is an intermediate level pattern since the rug maker needs to have enough practice that the stitches are absolutely even or the design is distorted.

I've made probably a dozen or more Star of Bethlehem rugs in various color combinations, most in the 36-inch size or larger. For the pattern to really show, that is about the minimum size, but chairpads or smaller rugs are good practice before making a large one.

Select the colors carefully for this rug, just as you would for a quilt. With fabrics of high contrast in color or tone, the geometry of the diamonds shows prominently. The rug on the next page (and on the cover) is this type.

For a more subtle (and sophisticated) look, choose fabrics that all have close tonal values, but different colors. The rug on the previous page shows this type of fabric selection.

The choice of color for the outside border is also important. A relatively light color will make the rug appear larger while a darker border frames the rug and defines its shape. Because of the visual impact of the design, a Star of Bethlehem rug will appear larger than it measures, so in a small room, a dark border works best while in a large room the a rug with a light border is more in scale visually.

For fabric planning purposes, I've used the guide on the following page for a 36-inch Star of Bethlehem, but there is nothing worse than running out of a fabric close to the end of rug so look at these numbers as minimums since your touch and mine will different.

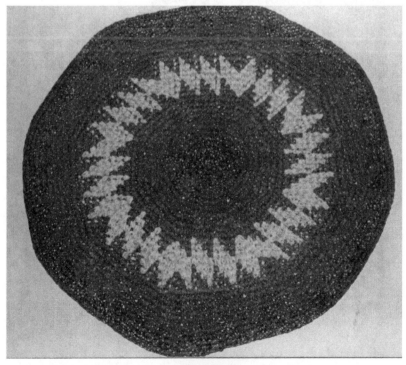

Star of Bethlehem, Charted Pattern for 36-inch Rug

Fabric Requirements in yards of 44- 45-inch wide fabric
(fabric is cut into 1-1/2 inch strips)

Central Star (2 yds); First row of diamonds (3 yds);
Second row (5 yds); Third row (7 yds);
Fourth row (9 yds); Fifth row (11 yds);
Border row (7 yds)
for a total of 44 yards of fabric.

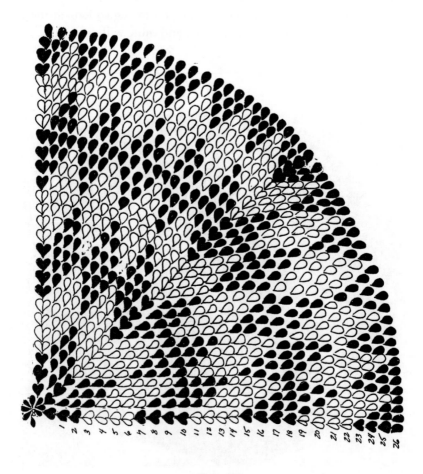

Reading a Pattern from a Photograph

If you've been following the progression of this book, by now you are probably able to look at many of the rug photographs and have a good idea how the rug is made. Below is a photograph of a "Primrose" pattern (an intermediate pattern using only two strands) and the original sketch I used to design the rug.

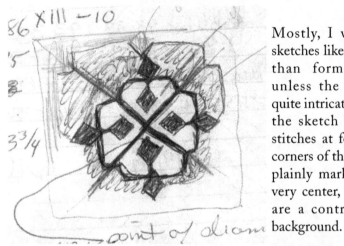

Mostly, I work from sketches like this, rather than formal charts, unless the pattern is quite intricate. Notice in the sketch the paired stitches at forming the corners of the square are plainly marked. In the very center, those pairs are a contrast to the background.

The next motif out from the center is a diamond in each quadrant which is followed by rounding to form a general heart shape, followed by a row of dark stitching. Look at the sketch where you can see the next diamond forming and the outer row of "petals".

Those petals are separated by diamonds also. and then a solid border around the entire rug. If you can see those shapes, you can "read" this rug's pattern.

This 30-inch rug took 9-1/2 yds for background; 4-1/4 yds for heart motifs; 6 yds for outer petals.

On this page are three more rugs, all intermediate patterns. Look at the photos to practice "reading" the rugs. Remember to begin by looking at the center and identifying the paired stitches.

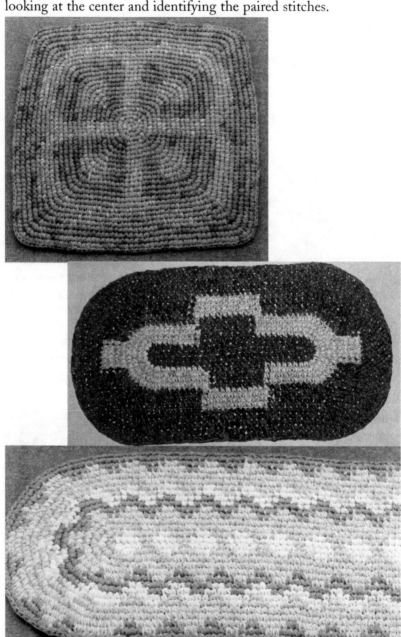

CHAPTER 14

ADVANCED
FABRIC TAPESTRY TECHNIQUES

When you are ready to take on more challenging designs in fabric tapestry, sooner or later you'll want to create a design that isn't symmetrical.

As an example of this sort of rug, I'll take you through the process that I used to create the "Zuni Eagle" rug in the round and square shapes. The design was inspired by the photograph (shown at right) of some Zuni beadwork in the book "American Indian Beadwork" by W. Ben Hunt, et. al., published by Collier Books in 1951.

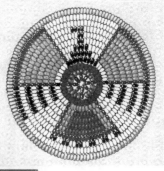

In looking at the beadwork, you can see that the design would lend itself to eight sections, making it perfect (I thought) for an octagonal rug as an asymmetrical design. In essence, I "read" the design in the same way discussed in the previous chapter. While the rug was ok, I thought (and it did sell for nice price), the distortion caused by the round shape, wasn't what I wanted.

(This 38-inch rug took 11-1/2 yds of the dark fabric and 7 yards of the light background.)

I re-read the design and translated it to a square rug with better symmetry.

(This 30-inch rug took 9.5 yds of dark and 11 yds of the background fabric.)

In similar fashion, I sketched this penguin in an oval shape. He would have had better symmetry as a rectangular rug, but the curved stitching gave his feet a festive look I decided, almost like he was dancing.

Other asymmetrical designs, from landscapes, flowers, trees and even a (sad-looking) horse, can work in fabric tapestry if you plan carefully.

Working from Sketches

Below is a page of design sketches that I used at our rug shops to help customers decide on motifs for custom rugs. Note that all of these are fairly basic, and an experienced rug maker can make a rug from any of these or other simplified sketches. Once you are familiar with the basics of rug construction, you can use simple sketches as your rug pattern. Note that the rug at the left uses the third design in the second row.

A collection of basic design motifs can be used for other applications as well. Above is rug I made to use in the rug shops as a sign. The center is charted letters (see the novice chapter) but the ends were made using a basic design from the previous page. Note the last one in the third row is a square, but in this rug, that design became the ends of the rectangle—making a very eye-catching sign.

Below is a Rose of Sharon design also from the sketch sheet. (This rug took 11 yards for the center and outer rose, 9.6 yds for the background, 3.6 yds for the middle rose and another 6.5 yds of dark fabric for the outline and corner details.

There comes a time when your plan for a rug is too elaborate to work from a simple sketch. That is when the blank charts at the back of the book will come in handy. This rug was inspired by a handweaving pattern for a blanket with two motifs— one I used for the ends of the oval and one for the sides. The intricacy of the pattern meant I had to use a chart to sketch the rug design which shown here, along with the completed rug.

This 27- by 56-inch oval used 12.5 yards of the dark fabric and 9 yards of the light fabric.

CHAPTER 15

ADAPTING CROCHETED AND FABRIC TAPESTRY PATTERNS TO OTHER MATERIALS

I've answered a lot of questions about rugs in the last quarter century, but some do stand out. One gal wrote that she had followed the directions "exactly" but the rug kept getting wavy. After several exchanges, I finally thought to ask her what she was using to crochet. It turned out that she was using ¾-inch strip instead of the 1.5 inch fabric strip that all of the directions called for. "I didn't think it would make any difference," was her explanation. However, it does make difference, and because there are so many different types of materials that can be used for crochet, I'm including a general guide here so that you can use them to crochet rugs.

The Geometry of Round Rugs

The reason that different materials use different increase patterns to make a round shape lies in basic geometry. The circumference (outside edge) of a circle is two times pi (3.14) time the radius. That means that (2 X 3.14 =) 6.28 generally works as the increase when the stitch width and height are the same. When crocheting with yarns, the hook controls the width and height so an increase of 6 stitches per round will mostly keep a crocheted yarn piece laying flat. However, with stiffer materials the stitch height is greater in proportion to the width so each round gains more distance and more increases are necessary.

Yarns

Almost any yarn can be used to crochet rugs, however using a single strand of yarn (unless it is super bulky) will make a finished piece that is an afghan or throw—not a rug. If you do use a single strand, choose a hook that will give you a nice snug stitch. For worsted weight yarn, that is usually a G-H-I size. The hook will determine the stitch size for yarn, so the rules of regular geometry apply (add six stitches in each round). The patterns in this book all show eight paired stitches, but you can adapt them to a single yarn by only repeating the patterns six times each round.

For making rugs, you will want to use multiple strands of yarn. Even rug yarn should be used doubled. For worsted yarns, use 4 to 6 strands at a time. Yarns that have stretch in them (most knitting yarns) will work if you increase six stitches per round.

Cotton yarns (such as "Sugar and Cream") do not have much stretch but will make nice rugs using a minimum of four strands. These types of yarns will require "almost" seven additional stitches per round. What do I mean by "almost"? The increase pattern of seven stitches per round will eventually cause the rug to start to wave. This is easily corrected if you watch your rug closely. As soon as you notice that the rug has begun to wave at the edge, make the next round without any increase stitches. Then return to the seven pairs in the following round.

The more strands of yarn that you use at one time, the more it will act like fabric strip. I once did an experiment to see how many strands of yarn were needed to make it work in the same increase pattern (8 pairs) as fabric strip. The answer was eight strands of yarn crocheted together were bulky enough to require the 8-increase per round.

Other Types of Cording

You can make crocheted rugs from many types of cording. Nylon utility cord (camping cord) and macrame cord are probably the most common, but jute an similar natural materials can also be used. For any type of cording, you will need to do a little experimentation. Begin a round using six paired stitches. Crochet several rounds to see if the rug "cups". If it does, start again using seven stitches. Most cording works with an increase pattern of between six and seven stitches per round, so if you use seven, you will need to watch for the rug to start to get wavy and then insert a round without any increases.

Thin Strips of Fabric

Many older crocheted rugs were made with very thin strips of torn fabric—usually recycled from clothing. These types of strips will stretch a little, so many of the old rugs were made based on an increase pattern of six stitches per round, just like yarns. When using thin strips (.5 to .75 inches) make a test piece using six stitches per round to see if the rug begins to cup. If it does, begin again with seven stitches per round, or alternate between six and seven increase stitches in the rounds.

Knit Fabrics

T-shirt knits and other single knits (usually cut 1 inch wide) will act very much like yarn because they have so much stretch. An increase of six stitches per round will usually work. Heavier knits can have an increase pattern of seven stitches, so watch your rug and let it tell you if six or seven works best.

Fleece Fabrics

These fabrics make fabulously soft crocheted rugs, but they are slippery! Don't use fleece on a slick floor unless you want the kids to rediscover the art of indoor surfing. Fleece rugs have a number of quirks, including "memory". If you lay a fleece rug on the floor with the "right" side up, and someone catches the edge, the edge will stay standing up in the air. For that reason, fleece rugs should be used with the "right" side down. Fleece is the heaviest knit that I've used in rugs, but its properties make it behave rather oddly and it doesn't cooperate in patterns that increase at an even rate. For that reason, I used a different approach to making round/oval fleece rugs, which follows.

A Different Approach to Round and Oval Rugs

This technique can be used with any stretch material, including yarns to maintain a round or oval shape. Instead of using the same number of increase stitches in every row, double up the increases in one row and use no increases (paired stitches) in the next row. For example, to begin a round rug using this technique:

Chain four, join to circle

Chain two, then Single Crochet into the circle for five stitches.

Working in a spiral, make six pairs of single crochet stitches in the next round (12 stitches).

Make twelve pairs of single crochet stitches (24 stitches)

Make a single crochet stitch in each space (24 stitches, no pairs)

Make twelve pairs of single crochet stitches, separated by a single crochet stitch (36 stitches)

Crochet a round with no pairs (36 stitches).

Make twelve pairs of single crochet stitches, separated by two individual single crochet stitches (48 stitches)

Crochet a round with no pairs (48 stitches)

The progression continues with twelve evenly spaced pairs in one round, and then crocheting the next round with no paired stitches at all.

For an oval, the same technique is used at the ends of the rugs. Alternate six pairs in one round with a round without pairs.

Making Square Corners with Alternate Materials

Curved edges (round, oval, heart, etc.) are really the "problem children" when working with alternate materials. All of the other shapes (square, rectangle, freeform shaping, etc.) can be made using the same increase patterns as are used for standard fabric strip.

When using lightweight materials (thin fabric or yarn) there is an alternate way to make square corners. Instead of using two paired stitches, at the corners, make a single crochet stitch, chain one, and another single crochet stitch. The following corners are placed in the chain space of the previous round. This alternate corner doesn't work well with heavy fabrics since it leaves a noticeable hole where the chain spaces are.

PART 2

HANDBOOK

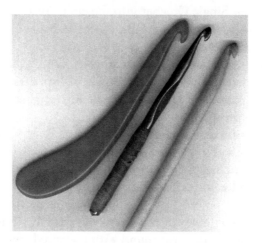

Tools

Crochet Hooks. For crocheted rugs, the first tool that comes to mind is a hook and the first question everyone asks is "what size should I use?" When working with fabric strip, you can use any size hook that is large enough to firmly grab the strip. The hook doesn't determine the stitch size, the fabric itself does. For many years, I used my trusty Boye "K" hook to work all weights of fabric from ½-inch strip to heavy wool. (Notice that the handle is wrapped with adhesive tape. It helps the grip, but also keeps the metal finish from wearing off under heavy use.)

Eventually I switched to a 10-inch wooden hook for a little extra length and in late years I've used the "Handy Hook" brand which has a broader handle and is easier to grip. There are many types of ergonomic hooks available and I do really suggest that you use one if you are planning on making crocheted rugs regularly. Rug making can be heavy work and we all get so antsy about seeing the rug coming together that we don't take the breaks from crocheting that we should. So, a little extra help from the hook itself will be a kindness to your hands.

Lacing Needles. For lacing in the very end of the strip and for finishing a crocheted rug, a lacing needle is the easiest tool to use. A bulky yarn needle, large size tapestry needle or any other large needle with a blunt tip works best. In a pinch, you can use a safety pin on the end of the fabric strip for the same purpose.

Cutting Tools. If you like the look and feel of torn fabric strips for your rugs, all you need is a pair of sharp sewing scissors. However, if you want to make the more professional-looking rugs with double-folded strip, you'll need equipment to cut a lot of strip efficiently. A rotary cutter and mat are the most flexible for that process. Get the largest size mat you can afford and a good clear plastic cutting guide to fit it. If you fold the fabric neatly into layers, you can cut a 5-yard strip from calico or 3-yard strip out of a single knit in a single pass. Even a whole twin sheet can be cut at once if it is arranged carefully.

Basic Sewing Tools. For the smoothest and most professional look in your rugs, cut strips should be sewn together (with the bias joint). A sewing machine makes the whole process faster than hand sewing. You will also need a needle and thread to tack down the ends of strips as you change colors.

Folding Tools. If you decide to make rugs as a business or to enter in a fair or contest, you'll want to double-fold your cotton and light wool strips. This process is made much easier with a pair of bias tape folders used in sequence. The folders need to be of the style that has a flat profile, such as the "Clover" brand. For fabric strip cut 1½ inches wide, you'll need one folder 25 mm size (1 inch) and a second folder 12 mm size (½ inch). The use of the folders is illustrated in the section on fabric preparation.

Fabric Selection and Preparation

Most of the rugs illustrated in this book are made using light to medium-heavy woven cotton and cotton-blend fabrics. These are the most adaptable to crocheted rugs and are widely available as new fabric, as mill ends and as recycled clothing or bedding. There really isn't a type of material that can't be used for rug making, if you handle them properly, but cottons continue to be the preferred material since they are washable.

Light Woven Cottons (Calico, Broadcloth, etc.) –Cut 1.5 inches wide for rugs.

Selecting cottons for rug making can be confusing since some fabrics will appear quite differently as yardage than they do in a finished rug. Remember that a rug will usually be seen at a distance of several feet, so stand back from a fabric to note how it appears. Notice how differently the two prints above appear when they are made into a rug. With a little practice you'll recognize good prints for rug making, but here is a general guide as you get started:

- Solid colors will accent the texture of the rug surface and rugs made with all solids will have a more sophisticated look than rugs with all print fabrics;
- Small closely spaced prints, like tiny florals will blend to an overall impression of a single color;
- Large all-over prints (like tropical florals) will give a general impression of tone (bright, dark, etc.) rather than of a particular color;
- Large widely spaced prints will create a speckled appearance in the rug;
- Watercolor prints will created a blended impression of tone and color;
- Plaids and windowpane prints will disguise the texture of the rug surface and give only a general impression of color.

Rug making is a way to solve those fabric mistakes that happen sometimes, since even large garish prints or designs will disappear in the rug, leaving only a general impression of the colors of the fabric in the finished rug.

Be warned, however, that if you're one of those people who take up rug making with the idea of finally using up that huge fabric "stash," that it has never happened yet. Once you start working with rugs, you'll be even more susceptible to the sale table at the fabric store. The prints that wouldn't have gotten a second glance before—no matter how cheap they were—are now going to be awfully tempting. You'll be able to see that the stuff that would be terrible for sewing would be just perfect for a rug.

Woven cotton fabrics can be torn or cut into strips for rug making. Tearing strips from light cottons is the quickest method by far. Pre-wash new fabrics before tearing to remove any sizing and soften the fabric. Rugs made with torn strips have a more informal appearance than those made with cut and double-folded strip, but the time saved in preparation may be important if you are making rugs for use around the house. Some people even prefer the look of torn strips as more old-fashioned or softer. This is purely a personal choice.

Single-knit Fabrics—Cut 1 inch wide for rugs. Single-knit fabrics can be used for crocheted and fabric tapestry rugs, but heed the advice about altering the increase pattern in Chapter 15. Most of these fabrics have a natural curl when they are cut into strips which makes the fabric preparation very easy (you don't have to fold the strip) and gives the rug a finished look.

When using knit fabrics, always test for the direction of the "curl". Most T-shirt fabrics are can be cut along the length of the goods (parallel to the selvage) or across the width of the fabric. Interestingly, the direction of cutting determines which side of the fabric will show when it curls up. Usually, knits cut width-wise will show the back of the fabric and knits cut lengthwise will show the front side. Cut a short test strip one inch wide. Stretch it gently to see if the edges will curl under and which side of the fabric shows. If it creates the effect you want, go ahead and cut all of your strips that way. If it doesn't, cut the other direction.

To make a single knit fabric strip curl up permanently, it needs to be stretched. A one-inch strip of knit fabric should be stretched to about 150% of its original length. For example, a two-foot section of strip should stretch to about three feet long. Don't overstretch knitted fabrics or the structure of the fabric itself will be weakened. Note that wider strips will stretch less and narrower strips will stretch more.

Occasionally single knits will only curl in one direction, so do a test cut both ways. (Some knit fabrics are heavily sized when they are new and may not curl at all until they are washed. If it won't curl at all, it is handled like a double-knit.)

Single knits can be cut as individual strips with scissors or a rotary cutter—don't try to tear knits. If you have cut the strips individually, join them end to end sewing the bias joint at right angles so that the seams are hidden. That will give the smoothest appearance in the rug. After they are stitched together, pull on the fabric strip firmly to make the strip curl up and hide the raw edges. If you have an ultra-modern décor, look for single knits with a shiny or metallic finish since they make extraordinarily eye-catching rugs.

Heavier and Lighter Knit Fabrics—Cut heavy knits 1 to 1.5 inches wide, cut very light knits 1 to 3 inches wide. Some sweatshirt knits, velours and velveteens will also curl, and will make for interesting rug surfaces. Fleece fabric can make very soft and durable rugs but needs to be handled differently than other heavy knits. Strips of fleece are cut 1 inch wide, using the circular cut technique (rather than cutting straight strips) because seams in the fleece are bulky and noticeable.

Very light knits can also be used—for example some sheer drapery fabrics. These light fabrics can be surprisingly durable in a rug, but don't plan to use them in a high traffic area since they will skid around and bunch up. Ideally they should be used only over a carpet.

Double-knit fabrics don't curl naturally and have to be handled like woven fabrics. The strips are cut individually and joined with the overlapping bias joint, or you can use the circular cutting technique used with fleece. In general double-knits should be cut one inch wide, but the heavier ones (and textured ones) often work best at ¾ inches or even ½ inch. Make a test piece with unusual double-knits to determine the cutting width.

The vintage polyester double-knits are often extremely durable and fade resistant so they do have their adherents. Other folks swear by rugs made with double-knits since they finally have something they can do just to use up the stuff, or recycle old clothing.

Wool Fabrics—Cut light wool 1.5 inches wide and heavy wool 1 inch wide. Wool fabric makes an extraordinary crocheted rug, but only light (skirt or suit weight) can be double-folded and used for fabric tapestry patterns. Heavier woolens are cut .75 to 1 inch wide and used unfolded. Above is a rug with light (double-folded) woolen strip in the center and heavy wool used for the outer rounds.

The best-looking wool rugs will use pre-folded strips to hide the raw edges, but even some skirt wool fabrics are too heavy to use with bias tape folders. Instead, the old pin-and-soak method is the most efficient. When I first came across this technique, I didn't really believe that it would work, but it does quite well. Cut light wool strips 1½ inches wide. Fold the edges to the center, then fold the strip in half to create the double-fold. Pin the folds in place with straight pins. Drop the pinned strip into cold water and let it get completely saturated. Note that woolens that have a lot of lanolin in them will want to float, so you'll have to push then under the water. I usually leave the strips in the cold water about 15 minutes to make sure that they get completely wetted. Pull the strip out of the water and hang it to completely dry. Once dry, the folds are set—but they aren't "permanent." If you aren't going to use the strip immediately, you can remove the pins and roll the strips into balls, making sure not to unfold the strip as you roll it.

Novelty Fabrics. Specialty fabrics can be used to achieve dramatic effects in rugs. Metallics, silks, linens, and upholstery fabrics can work well for rug surfaces and in wall hangings. Don't be afraid to experiment. The only practical consideration when using specialty fabrics is washability. If the rug will be subject to heavy soil, make sure to test wash all fabrics before using them. Shiny fabrics should be double-folded to accent their appearance. As a general rule, woven novelty fabrics can be handled like woven cottons and knitted novelties like cotton knit fabric. To estimate the fabric consumption for novelty fabrics, find a fabric above that is of about the same weight.

Denim, Canvas and Other Heavy Cotton Fabrics. Heavy cotton fabrics can be used for crocheted rugs, but they need to be cut ¾-inch wide and used unfolded. To minimize fraying these are the only types of fabrics to cut on the bias if desired.

Tearing vs. Cutting Fabrics

Woven cotton fabrics can be cut or torn to make strips for rugs. If you do not want to fold the strip for your rug, it is best to tear the fabric into strips after pre-washing it to remove the sizing. (Old clothing has already been washed, so it is ready to tear.) Just clip the edge of the fabric an inch or two down and hold the two sections apart and pull. The fabric should tear along a straight thread. (If it doesn't, the fabric is either too worn to use for rugs or is too loosely woven to tear.) After tearing remove any loose threads that cling to the strip.

Some "homespun" and tattersall types of fabrics are woven with a heavier cotton thread and some of them will tear and fold themselves if they are handled just right. Prewash the fabric. Make a tear for the first rug strip and if the edge of the strip wants to turn over, you're in luck. Make the next tear from the opposite end of the fabric to get the edges turning over to the same side. Finish tearing the strip alternating the end of the fabric from which the strip is torn each time.

Above is a photo of a "cooperative" homespun fabric that curled as it was torn. The lower strip shows a fabric that is too fragile to tear cleanly. Notice how the fabric has fractured and distorted. If you find a fabric looks like this after tearing, cut it instead.

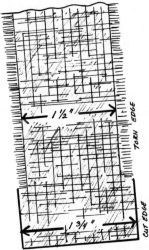

Adjusting for Cutting Loss. When some fabrics, especially those with a relatively low thread count, are torn, the loose threads at the edges need to be stripped so they don't tangle. In some fabrics this thread loss narrows the strip considerably. Measure the first torn strip to see if you need to adjust for the tearing loss to keep a standard strip width.

If you want to double-fold woven cotton fabric strip, the fabric should not be pre-washed before cutting since a little sizing helps the strip glide more smoothly through the folders. Strip should always be cut (not torn) if it is going to be folded.

Never cut light cotton fabrics on the bias (diagonal) for use in rug making. Bias-cut strips will stretch—even after the rug is completed—loosening the rug structure. The only time bias-cut strips are appropriate is when a very heavy fabric (denim, canvas, etc.) is being used for the rug.

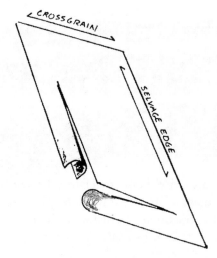

Cotton knit fabrics have to be cut since they won't tear cleanly. Before cutting, test for the direction of the curl in the fabric. Usually with single-knit fabrics, a lengthwise cut will curl up into a tube which shows the "right side" of the fabric, and cutting along the width will show the "wrong side" or back of the fabric.

If you want to use T-shirts for rugs and have the "right side" show, cut the shirt lengthwise (from hem to shoulder) and then join the strips using the regular bias joint. That will hide the seams in the finished strip when it curls up.

Heavy fabrics such as corduroy or wool may or may not tear cleanly, so you just have to test a strip of a particular fabric to find out. These types of fabrics really generate a lot of lint when torn, so it is best to do that outdoors.

Spiral Cutting. If you are using tubular material (old stockings, t-shirts or even plastic grocery sacks) use a spiral cut beginning at the edge and working around. This cut is illustrated with a stocking in the introduction to this book.

Circular Cutting. If you are using fleece or a heavy double-knit, or if you just want to make an old-style crocheted rug from recycled clothing, a circular cut is the one to use. For clothing scrap, trim any sharp corners to a rounded shape and then cut continuously in a circle until you reach the center. With old cotton skirts or shirts (woven) the old-style rugs were made with ¾-inch strip. (See Chapter 15 for the increases to use.)

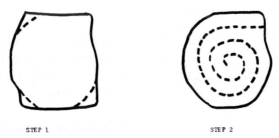

STEP 1   STEP 2

Circular Cutting for Rugs. Round off all sharp corners, except where the cutting begins, then cut continuously in a spiral toward the center of the fabric scrap. Use your thumb as a gauge to keep the cut strip in a fairly even width.

For fleece or heavy double-knit fabric, the circular cut can be used with pieces up to two yards long at a time. Work on as large a table as you have. Trim the corners to round them off and cut in a spiral around the edge. It is easiest to stand in one spot and turn the fabric around and around as you work.

The strip should be cut one inch wide and an efficient way to do that is to use your thumb as a gauge. Hold you thumb on a ruler and notice where the one inch mark is. For most women it is right at the first joint. If you are right handed, hold the fabric with your left thumb on top so that the end of you thumb is one inch in from the edge.

When using a circular cut on yardage, you will need to stop occasionally and re-cut the rounded shape at the corners. In the very center there will be two or three inches that just require too sharp a turn so discard that piece (or save it for some other craft).

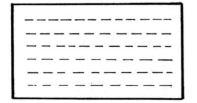

An alternate way to cut fabric or scrap clothing are short back and forth cuts which result in a continuous strip.

This technique is best used only on light fabrics and for fairly narrow strips (under 1/4-inch). There will be corners at each turning which can be trimmed off so they don't stick up in the rug.

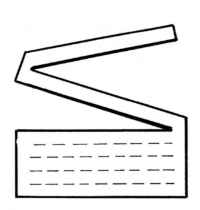

Joining Fabric Strips for Rug Making

For a smooth rug finish, you only want to use a bias joint when joining fabric strips end to end. It is the only joining method which spreads out the bulk of the seam and when the strip is folded, the raw edges are hidden within the strip. With print fabrics and those with an obvious right and wrong side, making this joint is pretty simple. If you are joining a solid color where the right and wrong sides of the fabric aren't obivous, you have to pay close attention to make sure that all the seams are to the same side.

The Bias Joint. This joining is used with strip that will be folded or curled into a tube. In sewing this joint the "right sides" of the fabric are placed together at right angles. A diagonal seam is sewn across the corner, and then clipped to a ¼-inch seam allowance. Notice that the seam is on the "wrong side" of the fabric. When the strip is folded (woven cottons) or curled (single-knit fabrics), the seam is hidden within the strip and is nearly invisible in the finished rug.

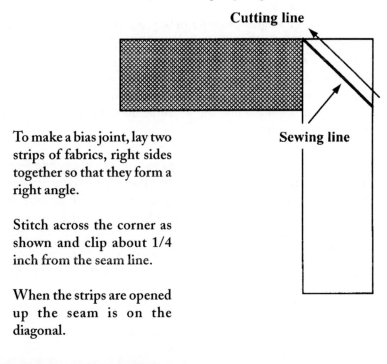

Cutting line

Sewing line

To make a bias joint, lay two strips of fabrics, right sides together so that they form a right angle.

Stitch across the corner as shown and clip about 1/4 inch from the seam line.

When the strips are opened up the seam is on the diagonal.

No-Sew Ways to Add Strip or Change Colors.

I've heard from many people who want to make crocheted rugs, but don't know how to sew or just don't want to take the time in fabric preparation for a "utility" rug. The easiest way to avoid sewing entirely is to have strips that are fairly long to start with (see circular cutting) or use fabric end rolls that are fifty yards or longer. When you come to the end of a section of fabric strip, leave at least six inches of "tail" beyond the last stitch. Begin crocheting with the next strip, also leaving a six inch tail. As you crochet, simply work over the two tails to hold them down. In use a rug will flatten out and the tails will be held fairly securely. If an end works up after washing, just tuck it back in.

Shorter lengths of strip can be joined without sewing, but the joinings will show. There are at least eight different slit-and-loop methods of splicing fabric strip, but there is only one—the bow tie joint—that doesn't result in a noticeably thick and lumpy knot, so that is the only one I recommend for making rugs. The bow tie joint is not as efficient as the bias joint, but it can be done anywhere using just a small pair of scissors.

Cut or tear cotton fabric strips one to 1½ inches wide—choose one width for the entire rug. You'll want the strips to be as long as you can get from the piece of fabric that you are using. At the ends of the strips to be joined, clip a tiny slit. The slit should be as small as possible—just large enough for another strip to pass through. Because the slit should be small, a pair of embroidery scissors or thread nippers is a good tool to use. Make sure that the end of the slit is at least an inch from the end of the strip.

Insert the end of the first strip into the slit in the second strip.

Then insert the end of the second strip through the slit in the first strip.

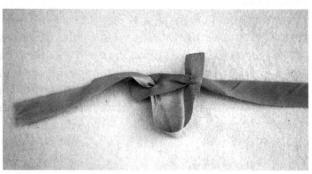

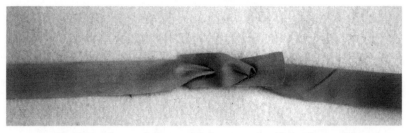

Pull gently to tighten the knot and adjust the strip ends so that they lay flat and curl around the strip forming a bow tie sort of shape. In making the rug, try to keep these ends laying flat against the strip. If you find that a corner sticks up anyway it can be clipped off—but only if it is a corner. If the whole end sticks up for some reason, it will need to be tucked back into the rug surface.

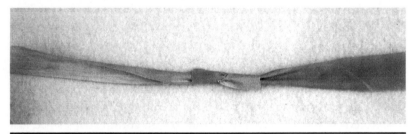

Double-folding Strips

If you want to make professional-looking rugs with woven cotton fabrics, you need to know how to double-fold the strips to hide the raw edges. Particularly if you are intending to sell your rugs, using folded strips will give you the greatest return for your time. The strip for some older rugs was ironed by hand which is quite time-consuming, but it does work. You'll be able to fold strip much more efficiently using a pair of bias tape folders.

Do not pre-wash fabrics that you plan to double-fold. For light cottons cut the fabric strip 1½ inches wide on the straight on the grain of the fabric (parallel to the selvage). Do not include the selvage in the cut strips since it has a different weight than the rest of the fabric. Never cut woven light cottons on the bias (diagonal) since the strip will continue to stretch even after the rug is made and the rug won't hold its shape well.

Cut the strips using scissors or a rotary cutter and mat. Then sew the strips into one continuous length using the regular "bias joint". Make sure that all of the seams are on the same side of solid color fabrics. With print fabrics, it is easy to sew the right sides together, but solid color fabrics are a different story and you have to watch the seams carefully.

The old fashioned-way of double-folding was simply to fold the edges to the center of the strip and then fold the strip in half and iron it by hand. I've seen yards and yards of this rug strip carefully put away for decades and it always amazes me how much labor must have gone into a rug with fabrics prepared this way.

When I first began rug making, I wasn't much more efficient. I would double-fold the fabric strip by hand and roll it into a tight ball. I'd discovered that you really didn't need to iron cotton strips since just heat would set the folds. So the hand-rolled balls went into the oven set on "Warm" for a couple of hours. This really only worked well with cotton and blends that were at least 70% cotton.

I knew there had to be a better way and by experimentation found that two bias tape folders used in sequence would double-fold fabric strip. These only work when the strip to be folded is fed perfectly straight through the folders. If you have a good friend or patient spouse or child, they can handle the feeding operation while you pull the strip through the folders and iron it or roll it up tightly. That works for a little while until your helper goes on strike.

Most of the time a rug maker will need to be able to handle the folding operation single-handedly which means you'll need some modest equipment. As you are starting, the easiest set up is to use a paper towel tube. As you sew the strips together wind them flat (no twists) onto the cardboard tube. When the strips are all rolled up, you'll need a spindle to put the tube onto. In a pinch, a broomstick handle will fit through the tube—just prop the ends of the broom between two kitchen chairs. The roll can be several feet from where you set up the folders. If you think you're going to be doing a lot of rug making, it is worth the time to make yourself a simple wooden stand like the one shown in the illustration. The uprights are cut out to hold a dowel, and the fabric strip can be rolled directly onto the dowel as shown or the dowel can hold a paper towel tube with the fabric strip on it. Just be sure not to twist the strip as you roll it onto the dowel or tube.

For strips 1.5 inches wide, you will want two bias tape folders—one inch (25 mm) and half-inch (12 mm) in size. Only use bias tape folders with a flat profile, not the round ones. The "Clover" brand of bias tape folders work great and are widely available in sewing and craft stores.

Next you'll need to secure the folders so that they don't move. If you're going to iron the strip as it comes out of the folders, this can be done with large safety pins set into an old ironing board cover. A more practical solution is to make a permanent folder-holder on a small piece of wood or paneling. Use a heavy fabric (like a scrap of denim) cut and inch or two wide.

Place the smallest folder in position on the board, lay the denim strip across it and thumbtack it to the board (or use a staple gun). The fabric sleeve should be tight enough to keep the folder from moving, and needs to be solidly connected to the board so that it won't work loose as you pull the strip through the folders. Then set the larger folder in place, immediately behind the smaller folder and make a sleeve for it just the same way.

Don't try to use a single sleeve for both folders since you'll need to be able to remove the folders individually in case of a jam. Your folding board can then be clamped to the ironing board. If you are just going to roll the strip into balls, the board can be clamped to a tabletop or other convenient spot.

Feed the strip from the roll straight through the folders *wrong side up* so that the seam allowances will be hidden within the folded strip. Then pull a length of strip through the folders and iron it or roll it up. If you feel like more tension is needed, set a heavy book or two on top of the strip just before it enters the folders.

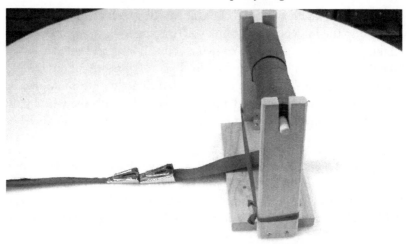

With the basic folding stand (shown above), note that there is a section of strip tied around the base. The fabric strip should be fed underneath the guide so that it comes off the roll at the base and can go straight into and through the folders.

Of course, over the years I've designed and built more and more elaborate folding apparatuses and each was at least some improvement in efficiency over the previous models. But the use of two bias tape folders together is still the basis for double-folding. There are all sorts of possibilities if you want to get creative, but complicated folding machinery isn't really necessary even if you plan to go into the rug-making business.

Calculating Fabric Yardage for Rugs

When I first began selling rugs commercially I kept detailed notes of every yard of strip used in every rug. I still have the notebooks from those days and reviewed them for this edition. For many of the rugs pictured you will see exact yardages of the fabric used in them, which I found in my old logs. Because running rug shops became so time-consuming I eventually stopped keeping detailed records when I discovered a simple trick. Ninety percent of the fabrics I was using for rugs weighed four ounces per yard. All I had to do was weigh the rug after it was finished to determine how much fabric went into it.

Those weights were much more efficient to use and the average became my standard for estimating fabric yardage. For crocheted rugs made with only one strand of fabric, 1.8 yards of 44-45-inch fabric was required for each square foot of finished rug. For fabric tapestry patterns 2 yards of fabric made a square foot. You can use these numbers to determine the fabric requirements for any size rug made with woven cottons such as calico or sheeting.

Since there are approximately four yards of fabric to the pound, if you are buying mill-end fabrics on rolls, figure that one pound will make about two square feet of finished rug. That, however does not allow any margin to compensate for unusable portions of the rolls (selvages, cutting waste, flaws, etc.), so if you are buying rolls you will have to cut to size, allow 10% to 15% for that loss.

Knit fabrics such as t-shirts or fleece, usually come in 60-inch widths. When cut into one-inch strips, they usually require one yard for each square foot of finished rug.

Heavier fabrics (denim, skirt or suit wool) will make more rug per yard simply because the stitches are significantly larger. With these sorts of fabrics, allow one yard (55-60 inch width) or one and a third yards (44-45 inch width).

To determine how much fabric of a given color you will need for a fabric tapestry pattern, you will need to count the number of stitches in a rug section. For round rugs, count only the stitches in 1/8 of the rug (one set of paired stitches up to the next pair) of each color. For square rugs, count the stitches of each color in ¼ of the rug. For round and ovals, also count the stitches along the sides.

Determine what percentage of the stitches are of any given color and multiply that by the total yardage you've calculated. For example, if your fabric tapestry rug has 10 square feet (multiplied by 2 yards per square foot), you will need 20 yards of fabric. If a particular color represents 20% of the stitches, you will need 4 yards of that color. When working with special order fabric tapestry rugs where I had to buy fabric specifically for a rug, I always added a significant fudge factor (10%-15%) to allow for cutting loss and other goofs.

Working with very narrow strip.

Because all of the rugs call for a standard strip with of 1.5 inches, you might think I am opposed to using narrower unfolded strip. That isn't the case. Narrow strip has its place for lightweight applications including light runners over carpet, placemats, table runners, etc. You can use modified rug patterns, including fabric tapestry patterns with ¾-inch cotton strip and create wonderful table decorations like the placemat and potholder shown. See Chapter 15 for how to modify rug patterns for narrow strip.

Working with wide cotton strip.

I've worked with prefolded strip up to two inches wide, most often using it for baskets in the shops, and it works quite well to add body to them. If you have a very light cotton fabric, cutting two inches wide is perfectly fine and it will double-fold and have good body in a rug. Unfortunately, there have been several craft booklets published which call for significantly wider cotton strips (3 to 5 inches). With strips that wide, the stitch size becomes so large that the rugs look coarse, no matter how nicely they are worked. The selling point for the wider strips was that they were "quick" and often the patterns called for using double-crochet stitches. Yes, they are quicker to crochet since there are fewer stitches, but the resulting rugs are often so thick that they present a tripping hazard, as well as the less-than-professional appearance.

Working over clothesline.
Crocheted rugs have been made over clothesline for a very long time and in the early days, it was a way to compensate for the thin, recycled rags that were used for the rugs. Unfortunately, cotton clothesline has a harder surface than the fabrics and the rugs wore through faster than those made solely with fabric strip. In addition, the cotton clothesline readily absorbs water and takes a long time to dry out, so rugs with the clothesline core were much more likely to develop mildew or rot.

If you do choose to work over clothesline, use a synthetic type that has a softer texture. (You should be able to squeeze it.) The synthetics don't hold water like the cotton clothesline and the softer texture minimizes the wearing. The best modern application for clothesline is in crocheted baskets where soft or slick fabrics may not have sufficient body. If you're going to use clothesline, start it on the first row beyond the center, not the very center of rug (which is worked over chain stitches) or the center will be noticeably more bulky than the rest of the basket or rug.

Working in three dimensions (basic baskets).
Crocheted or fabric tapestry baskets make lovely gifts and are quite simple to do. For the base of basket, use the same pattern as for the rug in the same shape. The rug patterns will create a flat base. When the flat portion is about ½ inch smaller than the size you want the basket to be, stop using the rug pattern increases, and just single crochet in every space around. Crochet as many rows as you like until the sides of the basket reach the desired height. Finish off with three slip stitches and work a whip stitch edge.

If you want the top of the basket to curve outward, make a round with increases, using the spacing of the next row in the rug pattern where you left off at the base, and then make at least one round without any paired stitches. For example, if you followed the rug pattern through row "4" for the base of the basket, then crocheted the sides without any increases, at the rim crochet row "5" to make the rim curve outward.

The same principle is used to make inner curves by skipping stitches, so baskets of almost any shape are possible.

Similarly, you can make crocheted and fabric tapestry totebags (from .75 inch strip). Begin with an oval or rectangular base and then crochet rounds without increases to form the bag itself. The handle is worked back and forth in rows of single crochet.

Edge finishes.
The edge of a rug is subject to the most wear so a simple finish with a whip stitch made with rug strip is not just a nice-looking finish, it also helps the rug to wear longer. Make the whip stitches in each crochet stitch, catch both top threads, all of the way around (including the slip stitches). This helps also to disguise where you ended the rug.

Scalloped edges are featured in some modern craft directions and while they can be showy, I haven't found them to be very practical. The scallops tend to catch as people walk on the rug and stand up. They also wear out more quickly because of that tendency. You can make a scallop of any width by using a progression of slip stitch, single crochet, half-double crochet, double-crochet (from 1 to 3 stitches), half-double, single crochet and slip stitch. The pattern is repeated around the rug.

A slightly different type of open edge is created by using filet crochet (double-crochet, chain stitch) for a full round. Then at least one row of single crochet around the outside to stabilize it. This edge is more practical than a scalloped edge and still very showy. (Finish with whip stitches.)

Making clean rounds without chaining up.
When crocheting wide bands of color in rugs, the color change is noticeable if you work in the spiral. (Take a look at the oval wide band rug in Chapter 5). If you want bands of color where the transition doesn't show, the technique is a little more complicated. To end the center band of color, make the change at the end of the oval by making three slip stitches. Cut off the end of the strip about six inches from the last stitch and pull it through.

Begin the second color at the opposite end of the oval with three slip stitches, and then crochet as usual for as many rounds as you like. End the second band at the same end of the oval as it was begun. For the third band of color, switch to the opposite end of the oval and begin it with three slip stitches. End the band at the same end of the oval, just as with the second band. You can add as many bands as you like this way, always switching ends of the rug as you begin a new band.

Caring for Crocheted and Fabric Tapestry Rugs.
As generations of homemakers have noticed, crocheted rugs have a dandy feature. The spaces between the stitches allow dirt to fall to the underside of the rug, leaving the top relatively untouched. The dirt collects under the rug and is easy to sweep up. However, don't allow your helpful spouse or kids to pick up the rug to demonstrate this feature to company. (Yes, it happened.)

In general use, a rug only needs to be shaken regularly (outside) to get the worst of the dirt. Vacuum a rug with the suction tool only, since the beater bar will wear on the surface of the rug. It is only when a rug is noticeably soiled that it should be washed.

If you use washable fabrics for your rug—and don't make it too large—the rug can be washed in a regular washing machine on the gentle cycle (no bleach). Most home machines will handle rugs under 36 inches and commercial machines, rugs to 48 inches. However, wet fabrics are subject to wear from agitators and the bar edges in commercial machines. It helps to wash them with a towel or two in the same load to minimize the wearing. Fleece rugs wash more easily since they are lighter and don't absorb as much water.

A safer method, which can be used with any size (and almost material) is to use the upholstery tool of a carpet cleaning machine. (Don't use the rotating brushes.) With soap in the machine and warm water, work the rug in both directions on both sides. For stubborn spots (especially grease spots on a kitchen rug) You can use a wet cloth and dishwashing liquid to scrub it (for wool rugs, use "Woolite" or a similar soap). Then use the carpet machine on the rinse with clear water. Rinse the rug twice to make sure that all of the soap residue is out since the residue will attract dirt and the rug will get soiled more quickly.

If the weather is nice, the easiest way to clean a rug is with a garden hose. You can lay it on grass or a clean flat surface. Use a power nozzle to wet the rug, a sponge and mild soapy water to scrub the surface and a power nozzle to rinse. Clean both sides making sure that all of the soap is rinsed out and let the rug dry out of direct sunlight. When it is nearly dry, the rug can be hung over a fence or a railing to finish drying completely.

With any wet-cleaning method, make sure the rug is thoroughly dry before using it.

Storing a rug.
There will be times when a rug needs to be stored away. Whether it is while you are working on it or the rug will be put in storage, never fold the rug up. Folding will stress the stitches and may cause stretching. Instead roll the rug with the right side out. For long term storage, be sure that the rug is clean and dry, so that it doesn't develop mildew or rot. Do not store a rug in a plastic bag. Instead use an old sheet or pillow cases, which will allow the rug to breathe.

The Business of Rug Making

Fairly often I hear from someone whose dream it is to become a professional rug maker and have a rug shop. They often have pretty romantic notions about what that involves. Luckily things have changed where a rug shop can be on the internet, or at craft shows and galleries, rather than paying the awful overhead for commercial space. But rug making is only one part of a rug business, under any circumstances. The biggest challenge for a successful business is pricing your rugs so that you are actually earning a decent living at it.

Inevitably, a novice-professional will compare his/her own rugs to those in home stores and undercharge for their work in the mistaken belief that they are in a price competition. That simply isn't so. A rug maker is in a quality competition and if you make quality rugs, you should charge higher prices. In checking my old notes, I came across the price data for many rugs that sold in our shops. I was astonished to see that I was getting so much better prices than what rug makers on the internet are charging today. For some of the rugs, I made three or four times as much money **20 years ago.**

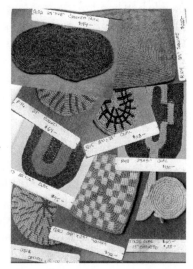

There is quite a difference in the quality of many rugs today (some would never have made it into our rug shops), but that is only a part of the picture. Years ago there were some basic principles that I learned about the profession of rug making, which I've condensed into fives rules that apply to all types of rugs.

RULE 1: LEARN YOUR CRAFT

I will never forget the words of an old German weaver (many, many) years ago. He said, **"Hand made should never look 'homemade'!"** This is a good rule to follow in rug making. Find a type of rug that attracts you (try out two or three), and **get very good at making them.** Learn how to do a professional job from fabric preparation to finishing. There are a good many second- and third-rate rugs that turn up at flea markets selling for a couple of dollars. If you want to make money from your craft, never settle for less than a first-rate product.

RULE 2: MAKE IT YOUR OWN

Make a type of rug that allows you to add your own creative touches. Think of yourself as a folk artist making one-of-a-kind rugs, rather than a "crafter" following the same path as thousands of other people. Allow yourself a training period to experiment with colors, fabrics, designs, shapes, etc. Some of your experiments will work great, and others won't, but you will get to the point where your rugs are a unique to you. One of the biggest mistakes that would-be rug makers commit is selecting a type of rug that is "fast and easy" thinking that they can churn out rugs like a factory. You can't. You'll get bored, your muscles will tire and you'll have trouble finding a market.

RULE 3: KNOW YOUR MARKET

You can't make a living as a rug maker unless you understand why people buy hand made rugs, spending a lot more money than for a rug of the same size at a discount store. There is an emotional appeal to the hand made rug that the mass produced rug will never have. When people purchase a hand made rug they will look for design, quality and a beautiful finish. If they look at your rug and say "I can go home and make that myself," you haven't put enough time into learning your craft.

You'll know you are becoming a real rug maker when people's reaction tend to be "How on earth did they make that?" or "I'd never be able to make a rug like that!" One of the best markets for hand made rugs is through reputable interior designers and decorators. These people are always on the look out for unique, hand made items. Visit several in the nearest city (and bring along examples of your work).

RULE 4: RESPECT YOUR OWN WORK

People see what they expect to see. If you try to sell your work where there are a lot of "crafty" items nearby, people will assume that there isn't anything particularly special about your work. On the other hand, if you market your rugs through craft or art galleries, museum shops or juried textile shows, people will assume that your rugs are indeed examples of folk art. In order to market your rugs successfully, you have to respect your own work enough to make sure that your rugs are sold in the right company. Part of respecting your own work is to price your rugs right. Keep track of how much your materials cost and how much time you spent to make the finished rug. Pay yourself a decent wage. When you add up how much the rug has to sell for you will probably be shocked, but remember you are not in competition with the discount stores.

THE BEST RUGS TO MAKE

For the best return on your efforts with traditional rugs, select techniques that allow you to work a pattern or design. These include wedge knitted rugs, fabric tapestry rugs, hooked rugs and their relatives, and shirred rugs. Stay away from techniques that only allow a hit or miss design or at best bands of colors. For example, if you want to braid rugs for profit, learn the wide braids (5 or more strands) which allow you to create a pattern in the rug. Another example would be the difference between crocheted and fabric tapestry rugs. Crocheted rugs are pretty common, but fabric tapestry rugs (which aren't any harder to make) will sell at about four times the price because they have a pattern worked in, making each one unique. Rugs made with woolens will command higher prices than rugs made with cottons.

After four years running retail rug shops, the pace became just too much and I switched over to selling rugs by mail and through decorators and art galleries. Even with the 40% gallery commission and the 50% decorator commission, I found that I was making as much net profit with a much more relaxed lifestyle. (With some decorators on the west coast, I made a good deal more profit since a 3' by 5' oval custom fabric tapestry rug would net $1200, rather than the $500 to $600 through regional decorators.)

Do I recommend starting up a rug shop? Yes, if... If you are really committed to the idea and have already made enough profession level rugs to stock the shop (minimum 50 rugs plus 50 small items such as baskets), why not? Especially if you live in a tourist area with other unique shops and can find a space to rent at a reasonable rate. Expect to work seven days a week or find a partner in a compatible art form who will share the space and expenses. In our rug shops, the crocheted and fabric tapestry rugs made up at least half of the inventory since they were such good sellers. So, if a rug shop is your dream, the rugs in this book will give you a good start.

RUGMAKING ETHICS & COPYRIGHTS

This book is as close to a pattern book as I've ever written. Usually my writing focuses on teaching basic techniques, which don't pose as many copyright problems. In the rug hooking world, there have been a number of recent efforts to enforce copyrighted rug designs, and I applaud their efforts to make sure that their artistic efforts are protected. Because of the controversies, however, I've had to clarify the ethics of rug making as well as the legal constraints of the copyright law for many rug makers.

Can I make the rugs in your books and sell the rugs myself?
Yes, of course you can. The books are written so that people can learn to make rugs, either for their personal use or to sell. What is protected by the copyright are the directions and the designs. For example, you can use the directions in the book to make rugs, but you can't copy the directions (or "edit" or "re-write" them) and sell them as your own property. The designs are also protected by copyright. You can make and sell rugs using any of the designs, but you can't pretend that the

design is your original design, even if you "adapted" it with some changes. It is also unethical to "rename" the designs to disguise their origins.

Can I copy material from the book to share with my craft group?
Short quotes from book are fine when used in a book review—for example a newsletter for your crochet friends. Anything else, including any complete pattern or set of directions requires written permission from us to reprint. That is why for the blank charts at the back of this book, each page specifically says that the chart is copyrighted, but it is ok to reproduce it for your own use. That's your written permission for those pages, and you can copy them as many times as you want as long as the copyright statement is on each copy.

Ethics in rug making extend further than the copyright laws as a matter of basic honesty. It is not ethical to learn a rug making technique from a book and then pretend that you discovered it. Too often the internet has led people to pretend that they have a "new" method of making rugs and they often rename it (sometimes after themselves) to deceive people into buying their particular rugs. That sort of behavior reflects badly on every rug maker and should be discouraged wherever it is found.

Blank Charts
On the following pages are blank charts that you can copy for your own use in rug making. Some of the charts are fairly small scale to use for sketching designs, while others are larger and presented in sections on several pages. These have to be copied and then taped together to form the entire rug pattern.

As this goes to print, it is our intention to have larger printable blank charts available on the "Rugmakers Homestead" website (www.rugmakershomestead.com) which you may find to be more convenient.

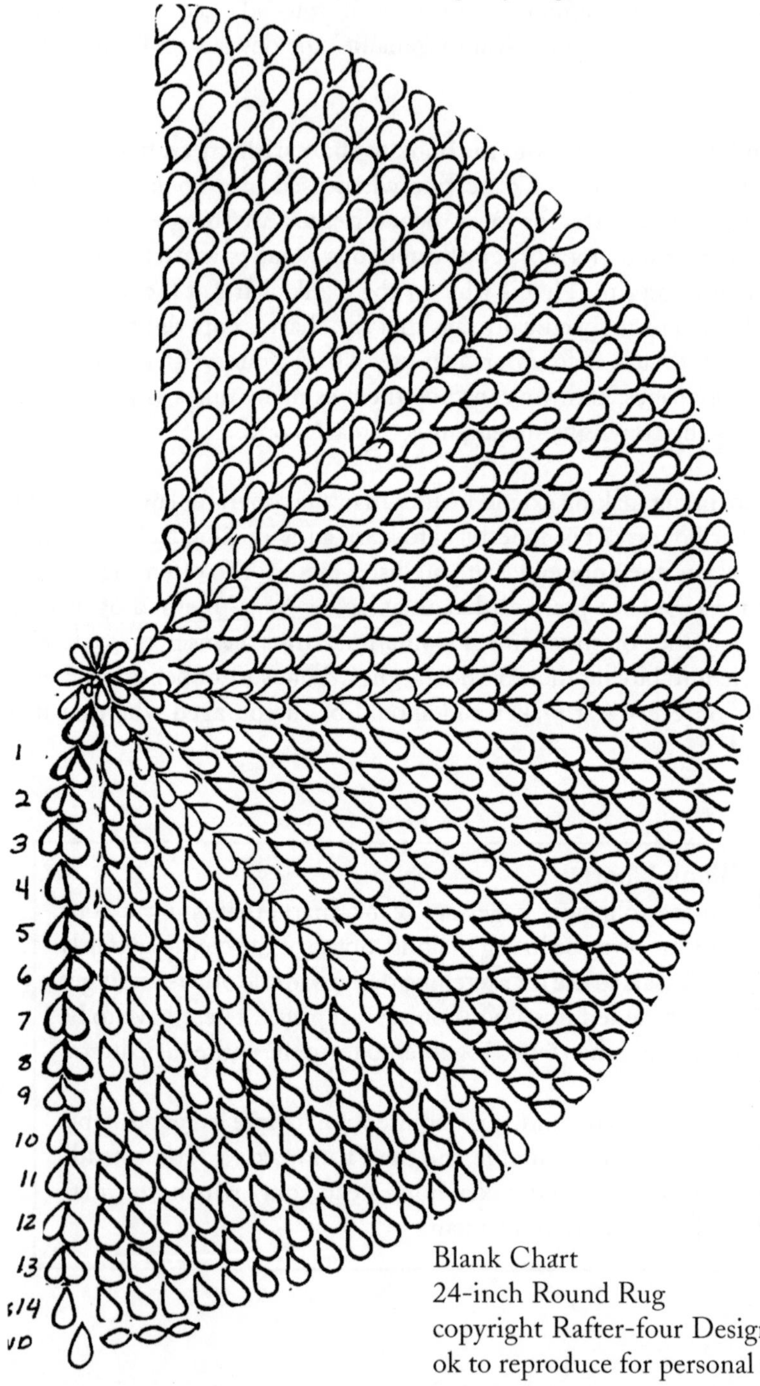

1
2
3
4
5
6
7
8
9
10
11
12
13
:14
ID

Blank Chart
24-inch Round Rug
copyright Rafter-four Designs
ok to reproduce for personal use

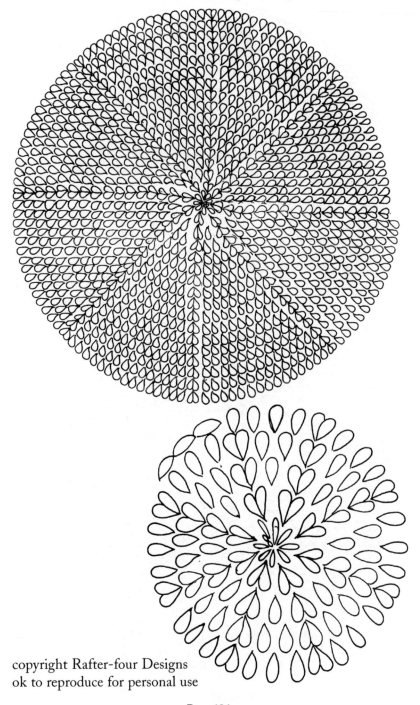

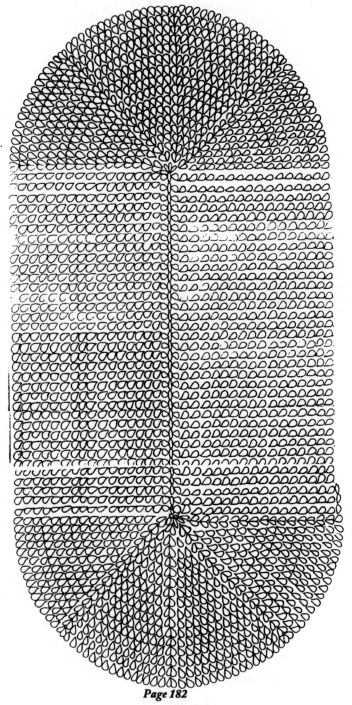

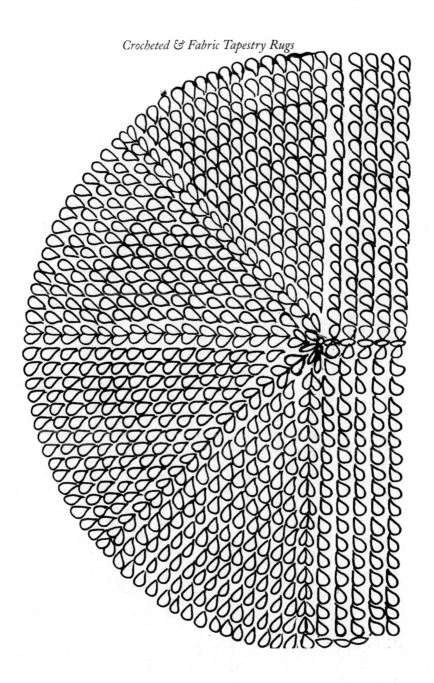

Page 183

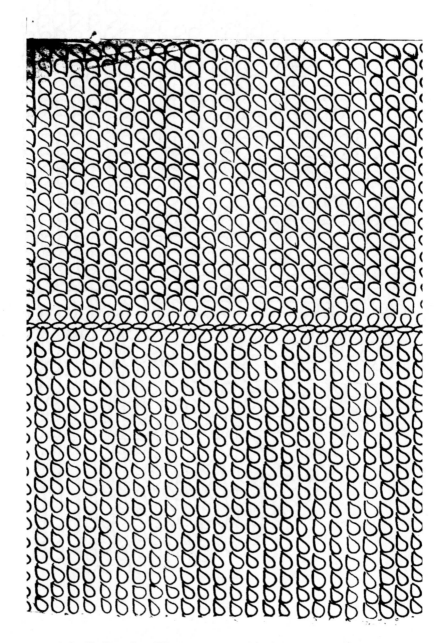

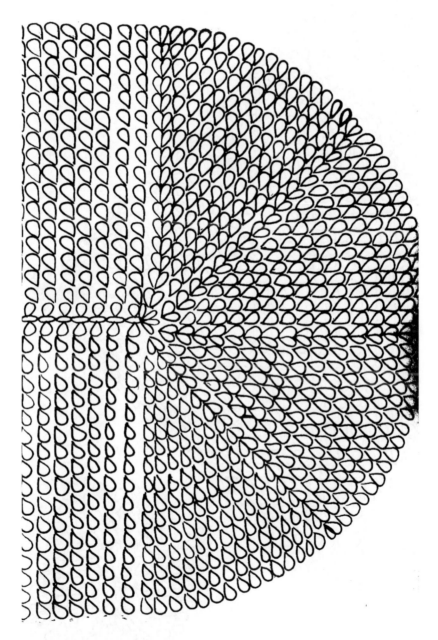

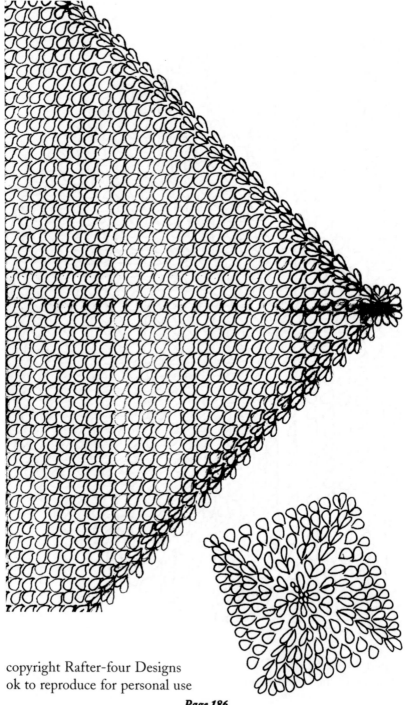

Resources

Rugmakers Homestead www.rugmakershomestead.com
The author's website with information about all types of rug making as well as tools and large-scale blank charts for crocheted and fabric tapestry rugs.

Inweave www.inweave.com
Raggedy Rugs www.raggedyrugs.com
Sources for mill end fabric by the pound for crocheted rugs.

Halcyon Yarn www.halcyonyarn.com
Top quality wool rug yarn, crochet hooks and other rug making supplies.

LACIS www.lacis.com
Crochet hooks and other rug making supplies.

Afterword

I suspect that there aren't many authors that ever feel that their book is "done," and I know very well that this book isn't because there is so much more I wanted to add when I ran out of room. After writing about crocheted rugs for 24 years, I had the fond hope that this book would cover them all. Well, it didn't, so I suspect there will be another volume soon or later.

In the meantime, I do hope that I've inspired your own textile explorations with this handbook and your curiosity about the field of rug making.

About the Author

Trained as a wildlife biologist and with a long family tradition of textile skills, Mrs. Gray has demonstrated a unique talent for researching and being able to reproduce old rug making techniques. Beginning in the 1970s she also experimented with new textile structures and in the 1980s began writing about rug making. When asked about her purpose in documenting the hundreds of rug making methods, she told the *Idaho Art's Journal* in 1987, "I am the door through which others will walk." Her goal has always been to teach others to make rugs and thereby preserve the methods for future generations. Mrs. Gray lives in the mountains of northern Idaho.

Lightning Source UK Ltd.
Milton Keynes UK
13 April 2010

152698UK00001B/61/P